Here Come the Kids!
Creating a Welcoming Community with Children's Sermons

By Steve Monhollen with Robb Carlson

23 Sample Sermons

NEW: Tips for Streaming Sermons

13 Ways to Avoid Zombifying Kids

For Sara Weatherman

Commissioned Minister of Christian Education

An inspiration and mentor in Robb's ministry journey.

For Sandy (of blessed memory), Jessica, Sofia, True, Rachel, and Isla,

Who taught and still teach Steve to see through children's eyes.

Separated by Covid, geography, and time; joined at the heart.

For Jeanne, loving and learning together.

Barbara Brown Taylor, Author of *An Altar in the World*

This engaging new resource isn't what you think—namely, a collection of someone else's sermons for you to read to the children in your church (whom you know better than anyone). Instead, it contains everything you need to create lively sermons that take your context, your voice, and your connection to your congregation into account. Steve Monhollen and Robb Carlson know what they are doing, and they do it very well.

Ola I. Harrison, Composer of "Restless Weaver"

I was overwhelmed by the depth of creativity. Rather than providing static scripts, *Here Come the Kids!* offers portals for the congregation's imagination to explore various themes of faith more deeply. The TREE model offered for preparing children's sermons provides an image of ministry with younger believers as tending God's garden of souls - a "cradle to beyond grave" project for the congregation.

Rev. Marsha Moors-Charles, Founding Pastor
Bluegrass United Church of Christ, Lexington, Kentucky

Monhollen and Carlson have done it. With their easily learned TREE model, pastors can develop authentic and deeply engaging children's sermons which will capture the imagination of not on our children, but our own faith journeys. I only wish such a resource had been available for me during my active ministry. You can bet I'll be passing this one along to my ministerial colleagues!

Tex Sample
Robert B. And Kathleen Rogers Professor Emeritus of Church and Society
Saint Paul School of Theology, Leadwood, Kansas
Pastor, Trinity United Methodist Church, Kansas City, Missouri

This wonderful book is what you need for children's sermons. It provides themes, resources, engagement, and evaluative approaches, along with delightful stories, important things to do and not to do (!), and ways to integrate the children's sermon not only with worship and the sermon but also with the larger mission of the church. Even more, the book provides a bibliography, online resources, and vital examples of children's sermons, that you can use directly or modify to make more specific to your own context. Beyond all these, it is simply a delightful read.

Rev. Erin Wathen, Author of *Resist and Persist: Faith and the Fight for Equality*
Pastor, Grace United Church of Christ, Louisville, Kentucky

We are all familiar with the often-stale children's moment: full of tropes, dad jokes, assumptions, and a general "dumbing down" of the adult message. *Here Come the Kids!* offers an antidote with a fresh take to rise above those old models. This resource covers the what, the why, and the how of crafting a timely and engaging message for our youngest churchgoers, without being too precious, or-—as the kids might say—"cringe."

Table of Contents

Sermon Themes and Context Notes

Beginning on page XX, you will find examples of children's sermons and related glimpses into the children's contexts organized by theme. The sermons are shown here in **bold type**; the contexts are shown in *italics*. Please use them as they are or adapt them as you choose.

Before You Start—Are you ready to relate to the children?

You may well be ready to provide a children's moment/sermon if you…

> …feel comfortable with yourself when you're around children.

> …look forward to being with the children and hearing their thoughts.

…are developing your own sense of wonder and awe about life.

> …can be vulnerable with the children and receive their words and actions as gifts.

> …hang out with kids and people who feel comfortable with them.

…prepare in advance for the children's moment, looking for ideas to engage them.

If you can be comfortable with yourself among children, then they will make room for you. And you can use this resource to strengthen your ability to be present in a sacred moment.

However, you may need to rethink whether you are ready to provide a children's moment if you…

…think of the children's moment as a task, a problem to be solved.

…habitually put off preparing until the last minute.

…think of ways to use the time with children to advertise a church event.

…use words too complex for kids without explaining them.

…feel anxious with the children and fill time with your own thoughts or moralizing.

If you think you're not quite ready, you could look at the first list above and the insights on forming a covenantal relationship on pages 14 to 18 below and do your best to catch the spirit of this sacred task. You might also enact the wonderful poem by Wendell Berry as a model for gaining comfort with yourself and what you may fear: *I Go Among Trees*. https://www.saltproject.org/progressive-christian-blog/2022/9/20/i-go-among-trees-by-wendellberry

Thank you for committing yourself to love people into life through offering children's moments.

Introduction

Children witness the full range of human experiences and can teach us how to live honestly and courageously if we let them.

Have you ever wondered why some children's sermons inspire kids and adults alike? We wondered, too. After hearing several inspiring children's sermons, we decided to try to picture "the thing with feathers that perches on the soul," aka hope. We are thinking of *hope* in the sense of *trust that leads to action*. We trust that we are a part of a sacred reality larger than we, that empowers us to love our neighbors as ourselves. We have seen how children's sermons can be an important means of catching what it is to love.

We created this resource to share the work of clergy who developed a covenant of belonging and care with children and adults.

The Title

You may wonder about the title. It represents our approach to children's sermons, which is akin to that of Robert Coles (1990) in his studies of children: "...a mixture of wry detachment and warm spirited interest" (p. xiii). "Here Come the Kids!!!" is a reminder of the unpredictable qualities of children, which we receive as gifts. Some of you may hear from church members a sense of yearning for a return of the kids. We chose the subtitle, "Creating Welcoming Community with Children's Sermons," to acknowledge that this resource offers some ideas about how to prepare to enter the habitat of children in worship and create a sphere in which to flourish.

A Structure

You'll learn a step-by-step model for creating a children's sermon that forms a covenant with the children and adults across time (See the section on Covenant below).

As Nate Miller, Dawn Renshaw, Ben Konecny, and Robb Carlson (from First Congregational churches in San José, California and Greeley, Colorado) described their process for creating a children's sermon, Steve thought of Abigail Johnson's book on shaping spiritual leaders in a congregation. Her sustaining question in planning is "What do you want to learn?" For our four clergy, this is a natural process rather than a technique that they apply. They did an excellent job describing a step-by-step process. Not an easy thing to do. (Try describing to someone what it is like to drive a stick shift car.) We developed an acronym of TREE (Theme, Resources, Engage, Evaluate) as a way to simplify your planning and preparation.

In our conversation about this, Barbara Brown Taylor suggested that, unlike a ladder, there are many ways to climb a tree.

Prepare to Climb a TREE

Below are definitions of the words in this acronym.

Theme. What is the one (and only one) thing you want to learn with the children (and invite the adults to hear)?

Resources. What things will you use to help you and the children (and adults) learn about the theme?

Engage. How will you use the resources to explore the theme with the children (and adults)?

Evaluate. How will you learn whether you connected with the children and what you might improve to connect better next time?

Sample Sermons

In addition to a structure and some advice for developing your own sermons, we have also included sample sermons for inspiration. Feel free to use them as they are or to change them as you wish. They are organized into five overarching themes based how they relate to expanding the world of children:

Belonging. Through inclusion in the worship service, with part of it consistently created just for them, children learn that they are part of something larger than themselves.

We hope that they will look forward to this special time and enjoy engaging with ideas, considering their values, and interacting with others.

Otherness. Children learn that there are other people in the world with interests and needs. Children learn ways to connect with and express love for others.

Spiritual. Children learn that there is more to life than we can see or understand. They learn that the sacred is part of everyday life that connects each of us to each other. They learn words the church uses to try to describe these experiences.

Worship. We provide children's sermons in worship, in part, so that children will know that they are part of a larger community of nurture. In a sense, we sing on behalf of those who are silenced by pain.

Humor. We think that, precisely because children experience great loss and sadness, it is important to provide occasions for laughter in church. In the sermons that follow, children will experience laughter: adults poking fun at themselves, playful interpretations that invite the insights of children, experiences that connect the tradition with enjoyment.

A Little Context

You will also find some stories and reflections sprinkled between the sermon examples. These are stories that connect us to the children's contexts and the influences of adults who invite them into life, sometimes in ways beyond their own knowing. Some stories amplify the preceding sermon, some give us glimpses of childhood, some show how adults are formed by their encounter with children, some offer metaphors of ministry to suggest ways to understand your work. Each one reminds us that we are in the midst of an unfolding mystery.

Resources

For further study, see the resources list at the end of this guide. We included a sample of books and sites that we used and found to be helpful.

Humility & Trepidation

As we wrote this guide, we did so with a major dose of humility and some trepidation. We have our limits and blind spots. Please note that this is not a comprehensive or systematic treatment of children's sermons. The examples included here inspired us. May you build upon what we have developed and create your own meaningful experiences.

Request

If you do nothing else with this resource, we hope you will look at the examples of children's sermons and the reflections and imagine your way into these moments with children.

We did our best to keep the following in mind:

- We kept one question as central: How can we invite children to become part of something larger than themselves in light of a covenant of care?

- We honor that First Congregational Church of San José, California and First Congregational Church of Greeley, Colorado let the children decide whether they wanted to come forward. For example, there were no age limits.

- We think it is important to receive another person with humility, making the person's narrative the central focus. Only if she/he/they note that they have been heard and empowered can one say that the encounter has been life-giving. The kids (and adults) will signal and even tell you when they have been heard.

- We did our best to focus on the perspectives and experiences of the children rather than place our expectations or interpretations on their experiences.

- We think that adults listening in will experience meaningful memories and insights, whether or not they have children or grandchildren present. Some adults hear kind words to children up front as if the message were the one they yearned to hear as children.

Two Quick, Quirky Quizzes

We know, here we are early on and there are quizzes already. Not to worry. No one needs to see your answers. There won't be any grades. But! They help with these two things:

1. How this resource can assist you, assuming you are comfortable with yourself among children.
2. Remembering kindness. (Yes, please.)

Quiz One: Is This Resource for Me?

You have the Children's Sermon this Sunday. Are you:

___ Deliberate in your planning?

___ Desperate in your preparation?

___ A bit of both?

If you chose any of these options, then this resource may be for you.

For the **Deliberate**, this guide provides a planning process that you can use to create and coordinate your children's sermons with worship themes, scripture, special emphases, and continuation in your church school and beyond.

For the **Desperate**, if you're in that Oh-my-God-it's-Saturday-and-I-have-the-$@%&-Children's-Sermon-tomorrow kinda mood, you'll find a guilt-free method to help you find an idea and then to build it into a more-than-halfway-decent children's sermon as part of creating a just and loving community...if you keep the children's lives as your primary resource.

For the **Bit of Both-ers**, this book provides a planning process and ideas to calm your anxious self, while not turning the children into zombies (more on that later).

We use the model, TREE, to create a template for planning: Theme, Resources, Engage, Evaluate.

We also urge you to follow another acronym: K.I.S.S.: Keep It Simple, Sweetie.

We think the theme and purpose of this resource are crucial:

- In a world that can be scary sometimes, we remind children that they are part of something larger than themselves that reminds them that they are loved and are called to love. All the rest is commentary.

- Plus, it's good for adults to be reminded of the spirits of children, including the sometimes-forgotten spirits of the children who still reside in us all.

The examples we've included here have inspired many people, and we hope they will be helpful for you, too.

Quiz Two: A Quick Quiz Calling Us to Kindness

Hold on to your heart; you're about to take a rough ride. The following (actual) children's sermon outline contains just about everything that will send children shrieking out of the sanctuary in search of a loving hug. You'll see moralizing, shaming, violent imagery, a potential assault with a deadly weapon, oh, and domination. Enjoy the quiz after the debacle.

Theme

What is the one (and only one) point you want to get across?

Be nice.

Resources

What resources will you use to convey the one point?

- Teenage son/daughter and children
- 2 x 4 board
- Hammer
- Nails

Engage

How will you involve the children in reviewing this one point? Actual narrative:

1. Who has been mean to someone this week? (The children suddenly look at the floor.)

2. No one? Come on. I know someone has.

3. Son/Daughter/Non-binary (named), I know you were mean to someone this week. Come up here. (Son/daughter casts a death ray look at mother.)

4. Okay. Take this hammer and drive a nail part way into this board.

5. Who else wants to drive a nail into the board? Be sure it only goes in part way.

6. So, when you are mean to someone, it is like putting a nail in their heart, just like this board.

7. Okay. Who wants to pull a nail from the board?

8. The nails are gone. See the holes?

9. When you are mean to someone, it leaves a hole in their heart that can't be patched.

10. So...be nice.

Evaluate

During—How will you learn whether the children got your one point?
After—How will you reinforce your one point beyond the children's sermon?

1. Will the children need a therapist to determine what point they learned from this?

   ____ Yes   ____ Maybe   ____ No

2. Should the teenage son/daughter/non-binary be rewarded for not storming out or yelling at the mom?

   ____ Yes   ____ Maybe   ____ No

3. Should the teachers, counselors, and ministers who were present have reported this sermon to DCFS?

   ____ Yes   ____ Maybe   ____ No

A Be-Kind-to-the-Giver Moment

We're sure the person who offered this children's sermon meant only good things for the children. We wish she had used encouragement rather than shame to make her point. We hope she'll move from moralizing ("Don't put holes in people's hearts") to empowering.

Maybe have a 2 x 4 with a couple of nails in it and several holes. Ask the children to imagine the things that mend us and other people when we are hurt or have hurt someone. Ask if there are people or animals or others who mend us. Invite them to put some wood putty in the holes; she could have her son/daughter/non-binary supervise that. Leave a hole or two and note that some wounds stay with us for a long time. Close with a repeat-after-me prayer giving thanks for all the menders in the world, including God's love.

Just a thought.

A Push and a Beckoning

As with many decisions, the one that led to creating this resource involved both a push and a beckoning. Steve was alarmed when he witnessed the children's sermon shown here and both he and Robb were beckoned to create a humane alternative by the sample sermons we've shared in this guide.

Anatomy of a Children's Sermon

No matter what we call them, children's sermons, integrated into part of a larger worship service, can offer a message that says:

- "You are a beloved part of our community."

- "You can express love to others."

If your children's moments are thoughtfully developed across time, the children and adults will enter a sphere of nurture, where they learn that they are a valuable part of the church who are loved just as they are. A good children's sermon will be shaped by the issues the children face in their lives. As you prepare, consider what the children bring to your encounter:

- Here they come, week after week, toddling, running, speed-walking, scurrying to the front of the sanctuary. Children from ages very young to whatever, alone or in tow.

- Or, they sit before a TV or computer, bouncing in anticipation or snuggling with a pet, parent, or stuffed animal, watching a part of Sunday worship created especially for them.

- They come expectantly, bringing a lifetime of experiences with them. Their concerns and language are concrete and often vivid:

"We have a new puppy!"

"My grampa died."

"I hope I don't get Covid."

"I love to be here!   "My friend said she doesn't like me anymore."

- They gather around you, trusting that you will welcome them and learn with them. What you do can be essential to their development and the well-being of adults who listen.

Adults often enjoy these moments, and they have an opportunity to overhear the Gospel and the day's message, as well. The best children's moment is akin to the early house gatherings of Jesus's followers: a refuge where trust is the central value and the unheard have a voice.

Getting Started – Okay. It's time to learn some steps for creating a children's sermon, starting on the next page.

What are the elements of a children's sermon/moment/time?

Here's a structure that we use and adapt as needed. We've included a few suggestions and examples.

Invitation

Here's an option for inviting children and adults into this element of worship: "Will the children please come forward? I invite the adults to pretend you are a kid and act as if you are listening to some really juicy gossip. After all, the Gospel is like good gossip; it is best when overheard."

Welcome

- Welcome the children by name if possible.
- Use positive language (example, "I am SO glad you are here!")
- Set a tone of trust.

Engagement

Here's where the content of the sermon, the presenter, and most importantly, the children interact. We've created a model for sermon planning with the headings Theme, Resources, Engage, and Evaluate (TREE). See the rest of this resource for notes on how to use this model.

Prayer

Here's an example of a repeat-after-me prayer at the end of the Children's Sermon:

1. Invite the children and adults to repeat after you the words of a prayer.
2. Include elements of the Children's Sermon in your prayer.
3. Use simple phrases, single words, and simple language.
4. Make it brief.
5. The example here is based on the theme: Jesus loving the children.

Thank you, God [Repeat]

For loving us and all your children. [Repeat]

For teaching us [Repeat]

To love each other. [Repeat]

Amen. [Repeat]

Leaving

Consider using a song as the children leave. First Congregational Church of Greeley, Colorado uses this one:

> Strong, gentle children,
>
> God made you beautiful,
>
> Gave you the wisdom and power you need;
>
> Speak in the stillness all you are longing for; Live
>
> out your calling to love and to lead.

Follow Up Options

Let church-school teachers know what your theme will be so they can integrate it into their lesson.

Include suggestions in the bulletin for how adults can reinforce the theme of the day.

How to Use This Resource

"People will care how much you know when they know how much you care."

If You Are Planning Ahead

1. Consider the worship theme for the Sunday you have the children's sermon. If you have multiple staff members, coordinate your work with the person doing the adult sermon.

2. Imagine your way into the life of each child you anticipate seeing. Where did you see them during the week? What might they be experiencing? What are their names? What do you know about their families?

3. You might think of some ways to involve the children in the process. Ask them to send you examples of things related to a particular sermon, for example.

4. Acquaint yourself with the Five Themes of this resource to see whether one of them will work for you. You might want to create your own. (See also Number 2, above.)

5. Look at the examples of children's sermons, especially the Engage sections, and imagine your way into these moments with children.

6. Read the "A Little Context" stories sprinkled throughout this book for a glimpse of why children's sermons matter and are so much more than technique, planning, and presentation.

7. Take the quizzes. They will help you to see if this field guide is for you.

8. After completing numbers 1 through 7, get acquainted with the planning model we call TREE. As you use this method, it will become second nature to you. You may find yourself imagining themes, spotting resources, and thinking of the children throughout the week.

Help! It's Saturday Night? Find me a Sermon!!!!!

9. (Please don't do this, but, of course, we are all human and events sometimes conspire.)

10. Still, it's Saturday night!

11. Do as much as possible on the Checklist on page 25.

12. Pick a sample sermon you think will fit and practice it a couple of times.

If you'd like to do further study, you'll find a list of resources at the end of this guide. It's not an exhaustive list, but we included those things that we have used and liked.

Notes on the Power of Wonder

Thoughts on Preparation by Dawn Grace Renshaw

A children's sermon is all about wondering.

Always have your radar on. What do kids wonder about? The questions need to be focused not on the kids but on wondering.

The children's sermon is a time to invite everyone to set aside preconceived notions about life and religion and open ourselves to this moment. It's as if we are all sharing in a secret, in a special time of wonder. It can be the freshest, richest, most authentic time of worship. The experience is not something you can put in the bulletin.

The people in the pews are like a silent Greek chorus. I always invite the adults to be like children, to be open to wonder about life through the encounter with children.

Preparation begins way before you get ready for a particular Sunday. Everywhere I go I am looking for things that I might wonder about with the children. How might this object or person or experience help us explore something together on a particular Sunday? What does it say about God's love or the human condition?

I had three purposes for the Children's Sermon. I wanted to let those who listened know that

1. You are welcome here.

2. You are enough.

3. God loves you and so do we.

You might think of three varieties of Children's Sermons modeled after the description of friendship:

There are friends for a reason, friends for a season, and friends for a lifetime.

1. So, there are Children's Sermons for a reason. To make meaning. To welcome.

2. And for a season. Particular holidays, for example. I work to make my presentation about holidays congruent with my theology rather than repeating a standard tradition.

3. For a lifetime. There may be life lessons that we can wonder about.

Story: The Central Energy of a Children's Sermon

As we prepare to learn how to craft a children's sermon, let's consider the importance of storytelling to the creation of our covenant.

Tex Sample (1994) writes that people create stories in the working-class sense of expanding the range of the empathic core, developing relational thinking, and creating a memorable base from which to address the issues we face. As you hang around children you may recognize how they function in an oral traditional culture, even as they are entering the world of written communication and thinking.

Tex's book shows and tells us how story, proverbs, and relational thinking address life's hardness, explore society's brokenness, and, in a sense, exorcize despair. He invites us to draw from the language styles of working-class culture to energize our storytelling. Consider the following examples as you prepare your children's sermon.

Oomph. You'll find phrases full of hyperbole: "She could start a fight in an empty room." Children often love exaggeration in a story.

Remembering. Memorization is "...a way to give people portable and lasting support. What you cannot remember in an oral culture, you cannot know."(13) Some churches use memory verses so that kids will have a stock of knowledge to support them as they face the unknown. If the memory verse isn't your thing, a children's sermon can introduce terms and stories that can provide similar support.

Relational/communal scenario thinking. You'll find people giving extra weight to how their decisions might impact a community. A children's sermon can tell stories, that, without being moralistic, can introduce behaviors that develop empathy.

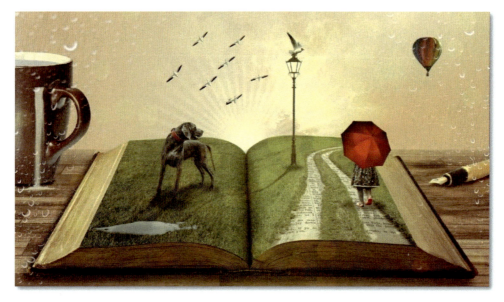

Covenant: More Than Show, Glow, and Go

We hope that the children's sermons help to develop trust, explore important themes of life and the church, and develop a community of worship. Over time, this practice helps to create a *covenant* between and among people in the community.

A *covenant* is not the same as a contract. A *covenant* is a noncommercial, nonpolitical commitment to the well-being of another person or persons, to

- Encourage each other to grow as humans,
- Honor the sacred gift of being received and encouraged,
- Trust and be trustworthy, and
- Love ourselves and others into life each day.

Below are encouragements from wise people for creating a covenant community.

- Use a Safe Church policy to create a culture that is trustworthy and accountable. See the Children and Trauma section of the Resources pages. The two churches mentioned in this resource use such a policy and practice.

- Spend time with the children in times other than during the sermons that you give for them.

- Greet them by name as they come forward.

- Laugh *with* rather than *at* them.

- Honor that they deal with real life issues of fear, loss, hope, love, disappointment, and more.

- Look at objects and situations throughout the week in terms of how you might include them in a children's sermon.

- Use self-deprecating humor. Kids love to see authority figures make mistakes.

- Speak to them as human beings, avoiding a sing-song voice. Just be a person.

- Aim to make one and only one point. AHEM! That's **one** and only **one** point.

- Keep It Simple, Sweetie (K.I.S.S.)

- Make your point vivid and on target by emphasizing one key word.

- Don't use the children as entertainment, as object lessons for the adults, or as a commercial.

- Choose questions that reinforce the theme. Be ready to offer some sample responses, if needed.

- Avoid starting a game in which you have the correct answer and the children must guess what it is.

- Relate the children's sermon to the overall worship theme or sermon theme.

- When dealing with *a painful issue*, focus on the support that is available to the children. Provide resources for parents and other adults who will be with the children. See Resources on page 86.

- Provide an uplifting conclusion that gives the children a supportive resource. For example, you are loved. You are not alone.

- Consider closing with a repeat-after-me prayer to reinforce the theme.

- Think of ways to connect the children's sermon with church school and with other times and places that are great for learning, such as home, school, or any time when they might have a moment for reflection.

- One minister noted that the staff agreed to spend as much time preparing for a children's sermon as they would for an adult sermon.

- Ask the question: How will what we are doing remind the children that they are part of something larger than themselves and that they are loved and are called to love?

- Use positive language. (See Notes for links to sites with ideas.)

Types of Questions to Structure a Covenant

Here are some examples of questions that can invite responses from children.

Consensus. When you expect the sermon theme will be easily accepted, then you can use **informational** questions: Who? What? Where? When? How?

Low Consensus. If, on the other hand, you don't think everyone will immediately nod along in acceptance, then provide a strong rationale. Use questions like: Why? So, what do you think? Why is that important to you, your family, the church, the community?

Rehearsal. To help the children remember the content and meaning behind the sermon, be sure to engage them. Here are a few ways to do that:

- Turn to one person near you and name things that are important about the theme (love, God, etc.).

- Ask the children to name as many things as they can that are related to the theme.

- Acknowledge their responses and compliment them for their memories.

Reminders Are Important

We know that we're repeating ourselves, but we're doing it anyway:

- In a world that can be scary sometimes, we remind children that they are loved and are called to love. All the rest is commentary.

- Plus, it's good for adults to be reminded of the spirits of children, including the sometimes-forgotten spirits of the children who still reside in them.

- The examples we've included later in this resource have inspired many people, and we hope that they will provide meaning for you as well.

Covenant: Some Clues that One Is Developing

Here are some clues (based on real events) from children, adults, and facilitators.

Clues from the Kids

1. The kids come running up for the Children's Sermon.

2. They are increasingly comfortable interacting.

3. They are learning the vocabulary you have been teaching.

4. They bring their ideas to you.

5. The children want to tell you things that are burningly important in their lives. These things are part of the pastoral loop of preaching.

    - Look! I have new shoes!

    - My daddy lost his job this morning and my mommy is mad.

    - I put a flashlight in my mouth, and it made my brain glow.

6. The children feel comfortable offering their own distinctive responses to your sermon:

    - Why do you think the people waved palm branches when Jesus entered Jerusalem? A child holds his nose, waves his palm branch, and says, "Because he was riding a donkey."

    - Why do you think the tomb was empty on Easter morning? "It was the zombie apocalypse!"

    - "Cut the peels off! The peels make my poops hard!" (When the minister shared an apple with the kids to illustrate the feeding of the 5,000.)

    - One Easter Sunday, Nate Miller took the kids into a giant cardboard enclosure on the chancel that was supposed to be the tomb. When everyone was inside, Nate said, "This is empty, just like it was on the first Easter." Whereupon a little boy piped up and could be heard over the PA system: "It's not empty. We're in here!"

    - When the minister showed the kids an enormous Hershey's bar in the bottom of a shopping bag and one little boy exclaimed into the minister's lapel mic: "That's the biggest f**king candy bar I've ever seen!!!!"

Clues from Adults

7. The adults are amused rather than horrified when their children say predictably unpredictable things—even if they use words we don't usually hear in church.

8. Adults who were shamed as children in church recount that they are beginning to see themselves through the eyes of this loving experience.

9. Adults say that they gained meaning from the children's sermon, sometimes more than from the adult sermon.

Clues from Yourself

10. You can flourish in a bubble of children at the front of the sanctuary.

11. You aren't afraid of yourself with children.

12. You are willing to let children lead you.

13. You are constantly looking at objects and situations and thinking, "I wonder how that would work in a children's sermon?" or "I can see using that in a children's sermon!"

How to Avoid Creating Zombie Children
Hint: Do the Opposite of the Things on this List!

Below are some wise insights in response to a question posted on Facebook: "What are things **not** to do with children during a children's sermon?"

These people know stuff. They give children's sermons, hear them, and, in at least one case, write short reflections in their journal until the children's sermon is over. Here they are, in no particular order (with slight editing for format).

- Speaking in theory and not being concrete. Patronizing them. Using the children's sermon to speak to the adults.

- Trying to make more than one point. I always make my message: God loves you and you know it because...

- Going too long. (Please...don't go too long.)

- Not using the kids' experiences to relate to them. If you fail to use their experiences, then they will lose interest. Kids have full lives, with complications and accomplishments. Acknowledge this.

- Speaking with them as if they are not actual humans.

- Treating the children as if they are entertainment for the adults.

- Only expecting the expected.

- Moralizing...bad.

- Laughing **at** them, patronizing them, expounding with words beyond them, not realizing how much they do understand.

- Using leading questions can confuse the children.

- Talking the whole time.

- Having the children face the congregation and having a microphone so you are sure to have the whole congregation hear their answers. (This is the **worst** practice IMO.)

- Using the children as a commercial for some church program.

A Model for Creating Your Sermon: Climbing a TREE

A children's sermon is a teaching and welcoming moment. It may have a longer-term effect than you can ever know.

To give you a structure for making planning easier, we offer this four-part process. To make it easy to remember, we'll use the acronym, TREE.

A TREE as a Central Planning Model

Here's the children's sermon planning model in a nutshell. We'll explain each of these elements on the following pages.

Theme   What is the one (*and only one*) point you want to get across?

Resources What resources will you use to convey this one point?

Engage   How will you involve the children in learning during your sermon?

Evaluate How will you be able to tell whether the children got the point? How will you reinforce this point beyond the children's sermon?

Using the TREE Model to Create Your Sermon

Here are a few more details about how to use each part of the TREE model. As you use this model across time, you'll find ways to adapt it to your needs and situation. The more you do this, the more it will become a part of you.

Theme

What is the one (and only one) point you want to get across?

Adult: "There's this animal I'm thinking about—bushy tail, climbs trees, stores nuts."

Child: "It sounds like a squirrel, but it's probably going to turn out to be Jesus!"

Identify a theme first. Use it to focus your preparation. Having only one theme can save you from meandering, going too long, getting confused, and/or creating zombified children.

How can you identify a theme?

- Connect with the scripture of the day, a holiday, a hymn, an event.

- Ask yourself, what is the one thing that I want to learn with the children?

- Collect ideas as you talk with people, read, watch TV, go for walks. Transfer these ideas to a document or notebook—one central place where you can go for inspiration when you need it.

Categories for Themes. There's no shortage of potential ideas for themes. To organize our ideas, we created five overall categories for themes that invite children to become a part of something larger than themselves: Belonging, Otherness, Spiritual, Nature of Worship, and Humor. On page 28, you'll find a chart that lists the sermons beneath the theme headings. We hope this will help you as you prepare.

Resources

What resources will you use to convey the one point?

Everyone in worship is the most important source of meaning. Build on their lives.

What else will help you to convey the one and only one theme? Here are some notions:

- A story or song.

- Decorations for a particular church holiday.

- Objects that fit the theme. For example, a two-by-four–inch board that the children can sign and include in the church's Habitat build.

Engage

How will you involve the children in reviewing this one point?

1. Connect the theme with the resources—with the children's help.

   - Make a plan for engaging the children.

   - Make a list of what you plan to do with them during the sermon.

2. Here are some ideas for engaging the children:

   - Focus attention on something in the sanctuary that fits with the theme.

   - If it's a holiday, ask them if they know what special thing is happening.

   - Tell them a (very short, possibly funny) self-critical story that will lead into the theme.

   - Ask them a "Who has…" question that will lead into the theme.

3. Here are some ways to redirect kids who are dominating or acting out:

   - We'll come back to you.

   - Now we'll let others talk.

   - Who else?

   - Let's talk about this on the way to our sacred circle after we leave the sanctuary.

Evaluate

During—How will you learn whether the children got your one point?
After—How will you reinforce your one point beyond the children's sermon?

During. Here are some ways to see how the children received the message:

- If you talked about a special word, ask them to remind you what it was.

- Ask them for ideas about what they can do with the theme at home or school.

- Figure out if you conveyed the one point to them. Here are some ways to check:

- Ask, "What's one word you heard that will stay with you?"

- Repeat the point and ask, "Thumbs up or thumbs down?" • Ask, "Who wants to tell us what the children's sermon was about?"

- Finish with a repeat-after-me prayer that reinforces the theme.

After. Plan how to reinforce your one point once the children's sermon is over. Here are some ways to do this:

- Coordinate with the teachers to ensure that your children's sermon theme is carried through into the day's Sunday school lesson. This will provide continuity and reinforce the children's sermon.

- If you emphasize a particular word or thought, you could post it in places around the church where children go.

- Give the children something to take with them that will remind them of the sermon.

- Consider how you might follow up with church-school teachers and parents to see how the one point may have resonated with the children later that same day or even a week or so after the children's sermon is over.

- Maybe, don't ask the parents, grandparents, and other adults in children's lives to do any follow-up on the children's sermons most of the time. Children are tested, measured, and held accountable at almost every turn of their lives. Church can provide a time and a place for them to have their own sphere of creativity and control. What might look chaotic to us is, instead, our children working out their relationships in the safety of a caring community. By letting them learn and absorb the message on their own (unless they ask us about it), we honor their process.

Note: For smaller congregations that can't afford to buy a curriculum, you could expand the children's sermon for the weekly lesson.

Pointers for Streaming or Video Presentations

Here are some tips, in no particular order, for creating and delivering streaming or video presentations:

1. Channel Mr. Rogers. Read about his approach to children. Watch some of his programs.

2. Make the presentation even simpler than normal.

   a. One point is still more than plenty.

   b. Know when to stop.

3. Some people start and end each children's sermon with a brief ritual, for example, singing, breathing, or repeating a saying.

4. Factor in time for children's responses, imagining what they might say in person.

   a. I'll bet you didn't expect that.

   b. Maybe you thought that we would…

   c. Have you ever…?

5. Somebody has to have the TV producer's hat on. After an early online sermon went off the rails, there were comments like, "Was anyone in charge of the technology?" The answer to that question should have been, "Yes."

6. Coordinate the children's sermon with the producer's focus.

   a. Make sure the producer knows what's coming.

   b. Decide ahead of time what will be on the screen.

   c. Be mindful of the camera's location. Stay in front of the camera unless you plan to be out of sight.

   d. When showing a prop, be sure that nothing is in the way of it (your head, for example) so that it's easy for the camera to zoom in.

Before & After Checklists

Before the Sermon: To-Do List

- Choose one theme.

- Check that the theme fits the overall worship theme.

- Gather resources and put them where you'll use them on Sunday.

- Think about which children might come and what their lives are like.

- Prepare open-ended questions.

- Ask yourself whether the children's sermon is a church commercial or more focused on the adults, then, if yes, change it to focus on the children.

- Coordinate well in advance any music additions with organist, choir director, pianist.

- Provide any slides, videos, or CDs you'll use to the AV person well in advance.

- Coordinate with the producer of the streaming video to be sure they know where to focus the camera.

- Stand/sit where you will give the sermon and practice it on Saturday and again Sunday morning.

- Practice using language that encourages. (See Resources for examples from teachers.) ✈

  Imagine welcoming each child, smiling, making eye contact.

- Do what you do (pray, meditate, breathe mindfully) to prepare to be present to the kids during sermon time.

- Coordinate with those who will integrate the theme into their teaching.

- Double-check the TREE process to make sure you're prepared.

- Theme

- Resources

- Engage

- Evaluate

After the Sermon: Did I...

- Stay with the theme?

- Wander a bit from the theme?

- Welcome the kids, smiling, making eye contact?

- Use positive language with the kids?

- Give the kids times to respond?

- Use humor that poked fun at myself?

- Laugh with rather than at the kids?

- Use the time to do a church commercial?

- Use the time to preach to adults?

- Coordinate well with... ✈ Musicians?

- Camera operator? ✈ Sound/AV person?

- Enter as fully as I could into the time with the kids?

- Ask someone I trust to tell me how I might strengthen my presentation?

- Compare what I did with the TREE model?

Sample Children's Sermons

WAIT! Did you skip all the good stuff about creating a welcoming community? Please don't. If nothing else, go back two pages and thoughtfully go through the To-Do List.

But before doing that, please take a slow, deep breath. Hold it. Now slowly exhale.

Now. Think about how people greet their doggies. "Such a GOOD boy! What a GOOOOD girl! Yes you ARE!" Now, ask somebody to greet you like that. Or you greet someone like that. Or look in a mirror and greet yourself that way.

That's the kind of spirit it takes to create a welcoming community using children's sermons. You don't have to act that goofy. It might startle the kids. Although if you involved them, it could make a pretty good sermon about loving and being loved or honoring the worth of each person.

Some of the puppies who come up for the children's sermons may not have heard a caring word all week. You can be the one to give them that gift...if you are willing to prepare and not rush this.

Better not to have a children's moment at all than to miss the chance to help the children catch that they are loved and loving.

You're the one to do this. Yes you ARE!!!

Now...please go back two pages and complete the checklist. You'll be glad you did.

Note: Please, please use and adapt whatever you like from this resource. You might give a nod to our work so we feel good, and, more importantly, so others can find this resource, too.

Theme: Belonging

You are welcome here!

You are loved!

You are able to share love with others!

Together Apart

Useful when the scripture focuses on loss and hope or the children have recently experienced disappointment.

This sermon was originally given as a streaming presentation, but you can adapt it for in-person use. For example, add questions and invite the children to help.

Theme

We can start over...with a little help.

Resources

Children's building blocks

Engage

1. Start stacking one block atop another, making a tower.
    - "Hi, Kids. I'm working on finishing up this tower.
    - I'm down to the very last block.
    - There! I'm finished!"
2. The tower falls over.
    - "Well, that's disappointing.
    - I spent so much time on that and then it got wrecked.
    - I feel a little angry. Sad, too.
        - I wonder if you might experience this sometimes too.
3. Look! All the blocks I used are still there.
    - We have something to use.
    - We can still try again.
4. I guess being Together Apart is normal.
    - We can just try again.
    - What people might help you? Can you help someone else try again?

Evaluate

5. Do you have something that has Together Apart you?
6. Can you try to do it again?
7. Is there someone who could help you?
8. Repeat-after-me prayer:
    - O, God.
    - Sometimes we get Together Apart.
    - We might feel sad and angry.
    - Thank you that we can try again
    - Thank you for people who help us.
    - Amen.

A Little Context—Keepers of the Fabric

When the great cathedrals were being built in England beginning in the 12th and 13th centuries (for example, Salisbury Cathedral shown here, built from 1220 to 1258 CE; Spire 1361 CE), one role was of particular importance. Spelled variously in Latin, the term *custos fabricus* describes the keeper (*custos*) of the fabric (*fabricus*). (See *The Pillars of the Earth* by Ken Follett.)

The keeper of the fabric kept an overview of the whole project, making rounds to assure that adequate materials and workers were available, progress moved at an appropriate pace, and the morale of the workers remained focused on the grand construction that would be finished in another lifetime. Once the cathedral was completed, the keeper of the fabric assured the good repair of the grand structure.

We regularly use various everyday metaphors for the care of communities through ministry: shepherd (sheep herder), minister (minus/lesser), pastor (feeder). As a keeper of the fabric, each of us looks after the physical, emotional, and spiritual well-being of those with whom we are entrusted (including our own). As a church, we combine our gifts as keepers of the fabric of God's beloved community (humanity and the earth).

Your work with children's sermons allows you to keep and mend the fabric of the lives of children (and adults) in and beyond the congregation.

Have Courage

Useful when there are times of crisis or during important transitions, such as starting school or moving.

Theme

"Be of good cheer." John 16:33

"I am Somebody," a poem used by Rev. Jesse Jackson on Sesame Street and at the beginning of meetings of PUSH-Excel, a program to motivate Black students.

Engage

1. "Sometimes I feel very small and like I am carrying a heavy weight. Do any of you ever feel like that? Should we ask the adults if they do?"
2. "It could be that something painful happened and I don't know what to do."
3. There was a minister named Rev. Jesse Jackson who used to lead children in a poem that they could use when they felt small. Would you like to learn it?
4. Okay. It's a repeat-after-me poem. Here goes:
   - I am!
   - Somebody!
   - I AM!
   - Somebody!
   - I may get scared!
   - I may feel tiny!
   - But I AM!
   - God's child.
   - I AM!
   - Somebody!
5. Would you like to invite the adults to join us?
   - Have the kids lead the call and response at first.
   - You can adapt this to whatever situation you face.
6. This is like when Jesus said to his disciples, "Things get rough. Have courage. Be of good cheer!" (John 16:33)
7. Can you say that?
   - Things get rough.
   - Have courage!
   - Be of good cheer!

Evaluate

8. Repeat-after-me prayer giving thanks for courage and support.

A Little Context— In the Beginning Is the Question

As the sermon above illustrates, children declare their great "I am!" at an early age. Their life at church can be an important way for them to strengthen their sense of self and connection.

Long ago, in a far-off place, Steve experienced a formative encounter with his older daughter.

He remembers: It was a Saturday like any other as I strolled into the playroom. "Lunchtime," I beckoned our two-year old first born. Ordinarily she would have jumped up and, arms aflutter to stay balanced, scurried into the kitchen.

Not on this day. Her eyes signaled to me that our relationship was about to take an important turn.

"Why?" she inquired.

"Hmmm," thought I, responding with, "So you can get food to give you energy to play."

"Why?" came her response.

And suddenly I was in a room of fear, which had morphed into a mostly dark courtroom with a spotlight in my eyes. I was the defendant as this small, determined person brought the full force of her cross examination to lead me to my inevitable doom. The burden of proof was on my head. "Couldn't I get a temporary restraining order so we can have lunch?" I wondered.

I tried again. "Would you like to see what yummy things are waiting for you to eat?"

She stood with straightened back and struck a posture that would do Wonder Woman proud, "WHY?!"

It was as if we were witnessing, participating in a creation story, where chaos mixes with a yearning to hear the words, "Let there be me!"

And this powerful person before me wasn't asking me to treat her as a problem to be solved. I saw her wanting me to honor her as a mystery who was and is unfolding. A mystery like all parts of creation, who asserts, "I am! I can be no other. Help me honor that unfolding."

It was as if her entreaty, "Why?" was a prologue to a life at its beginning, which is each of our lives in all our endings and beginnings. I thought of it like this:

In the beginning was the question and the question was with wonder and the question was wonder. Life came into being because of this wonder. And we beheld its glory, full of trust and yearning. And the world received it not.

So, we create worlds, like church, that at our best receive, nurture, and express this wonder and awe.

And that long-ago day became sacred for that novice parent. The memory of it is still sacred.

Ruach—The Breath of God

Useful when...there is a baptism, a time of transition (farewell, starting school, installing a minister), special blessing times (teachers, members going on service trip).

Theme

The Breath of God Breathes through each one of us.

Resources

- Genesis 1:2—The *Ruach* of God blew over the chaotic waters
- Examples of the Breath of God (See the examples after the end of this sermon.)
- An event that invites talking about the Breath of God, for example, a baptism, a group taking water to refugees, or someone leaving home

Engage

1. *Ruach*. Can you say that word? Ru-ach (Roo-ahk). That's our word for today. *Ruach*.

    - It's in the Hebrew language, and it's used in the Bible.
    - Genesis 1:2—The Ruach of God blew over the chaotic waters.
    - It can mean three things: Wind, Breath, Spirit. *Ruach.*

2. Where do you think this Wind, this Breath, this Spirit blows? (See example sheet for ideas)

    - In the trees?
    - Where else?
    - Do you think it can blow through you, through me, through each of us?

3. What do you think this Breath of God would want us to know?

    - We are loved?
    - We can be loving? What else?

4. We are about to baptize (name of person), and we need your help. Would you gently blow your breath on the baptismal waters as a blessing for this child? As a gift to this child and family? By doing this, we're saying: You are loved. You are loving. Together we can be loving.

5. Take the bowl to each cluster of children and ask them to gently blow the Breath of God.

    - Is there anyone else in this place who also breathes the Breath of God?
    - Should we invite them to join us?

6. Hold the bowl toward the choir, then toward the nave.

7. Perform the baptism.

8. As the parents/child remain, conclude the children's sermon with the evaluation section on the next page.

Evaluate

9. What is the word you will remember today? *Ruach*

10. What does it mean? Wind, Breath, Spirit

Page 32

11. . How can you use what you have learned?

  - Can you bless yourself in the mirror in the morning?
  - Can you bless your sister or brother? Your mom and dad? A friend?
  - Your teacher? Someone who is mean to you? Someone you don't like?

12.   Conclude with a repeat-after-me prayer.

13. If the children leave for church school, begin the gathering by reinforcing the theme, or focus the entire class on the theme.

A Little Context—Examples of God's Breath

Notes on God's Breath by Dave Monhollen

You can ask yourself ahead of time and the children during the sermon, "When has God breathed on you recently?" Here are some examples for children, who can add their own examples:

- When you sit with Mom or Dad all snuggled in a chair or on the couch as they read your favorite book; that's God breathing on you.

- When you are tucked safely into bed and feel all warm and loved as you are kissed good night, that's God breathing on you.

- When you're rolling around on the floor with your brother or sister or Mom or Dad, laughing so hard you can hardly breathe, that's God breathing on you.

- When a cute puppy runs to you all wiggly and smiling that puppy smile and you drop down on the ground and pick it up and it plants puppy kisses all over your face with its tongue— yuk, that's God breathing on you.

- When you've fallen down and bumped your knee hard and you go crying to Mom and she dries your tears, cleans your knee and places a gentle kiss on it and says, It's going to be all right, it's just a bruise, that's God breathing on you.

- When you are walking through the forest or along a stream or the ocean and see and smell the beautiful flowers, or you hear the birds singing and flying, or you run at the edge of the beach or wade in a stream and it seems like magic, that's God breathing on you.

- When you get to hold a little baby for the first time and touch its little fingers and it holds your finger and feels so soft and warm, that's God breathing on you.

- When you reassure a friend or help someone, say a prayer of thanks, or listen to a friend, you give God's breath of love to someone else.

- When there are things you don't understand and hurts or losses you don't know how to deal with it's also going to be OK because God is always breathing on you.

- When has God breathed on you recently?

Scary Times and Safe People

Useful when...the community has experienced a widely known trauma. When the scripture addresses loss and hope.

Theme

You are loved just the way you are.

Resources

- Information in program for parents and supportive adults (See the Resources section on Trauma and Children.)

- Possible text: Matthew 19:14—And Jesus said, "Let the children come to me; do not get in their way. For the kingdom of heaven belongs to children like these."

- Note: There's a wonderful book called "*A Terrible Thing Happened*," by Margaret M. Holmes. It would be great for reinforcing this sermon in church-school classes. (It's comforting for adults, too.)

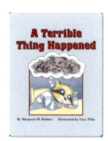

You might also look at *The Invisible String* by Patrice Karst, which emphasizes the strings of love that connect us all.

Engage

1. Do you think grownups ever get scared? (Ask adults who have been scared to raise their hands.)

2. Ask, "When I was your age and became scared, what do you think I would do?" Invite ideas.

   - Agree with some of the things. Or, say something like, "I didn't think of that, but it would have been a good idea."

   - Maybe add something from your own experience.

3. What kinds of things scare kids these days? Affirm each thing.

4. Do you think grownups were scared when they were kids? What about now? Should we ask them?

5. To adults: If you are comfortable telling us, please raise your hand if you get scared sometimes.

   - What kinds of things can we do when we are scared?

   - Acknowledge their ideas.

   - Make sure these ideas are included: Look for helpful people. Also, what about animals? They will remind you that you are safe.

6. Remember when we learned about Breathing the Breath of God to bless someone? Do you think that might be something we could do during scary times?

7.   There's a scripture that I think of when scary things happen. Maybe you've heard it; it's from Matthew 19:14. "And Jesus said, Let the children come to me; do not get in their way. For the kingdom of heaven belongs to children like these."

- If we are followers of Jesus, then whom would we welcome?

- Invite and affirm their answers.

8.   Who else? Add any groups you want to be sure they include.

Evaluate

9.   So, do you think everybody gets scared sometimes?

10. Please remember that you are loved in scary times and regular times.

11. Would you join me in a repeat-after-me prayer?

- Give thanks for love and helpful people.

- Give thanks, also, because we are loved in scary times and in regular times.

A Little Context—A Helping Witness

As the sermon above explores, children can be reassured that they are not alone, even in the worst of times.

Dr. Alice Miller, whose seminal work focused on the impact of parental child abuse, notes how having a helpful witness to a child's suffering, even later in adulthood, can transform a person. Her excellent post, "The Essential Role of an Enlightened Witness in Society," is replete with insights about the importance that one person can have to help a child (or an adult) catch a notion of trust and of love.

Who can know which of the children with you are struggling with very painful circumstances? Or which adults still carry the wounds of their childhood? You have the opportunity to be an enlightened witness for them.

https://www.alice-miller.com/en/the-essential-role-of-an-enlightened-witness-in-society-2/

Sometimes You Feel Like a Dot

This sermon works well for a streaming service. You can record it ahead of time and share it when needed.

Useful when…the scripture emphasizes how even the least of us have a contribution to make

Theme

God uses even tiny moments and seemingly small people to create a large and caring community.

Resources

- A large mural made with dots or short brush strokes.

- Camera for recording

Engage

1. Stand right next to the mural.

    - Hi, Kids! During our Covid separation, I'm spending more time with my dog, Zaley.

    - Today we've found this wall with a bunch of dots.

    - Seems kinda odd to just put dots on the side of a wall.

2. I'm finding that because my life has slowed down, I notice more tiny moments. Like how Zaley looks at me when she wants to play, or is feeling sad, or shows me she loves me.

3. What happens when we move away from these dots on the wall? All the little things begin to add up to a big thing, a big picture. The dots grow into a picture.

4. It's like that with God. God uses all the little things in our lives—and each of us— even if we feel like a dot. God uses us for a part of a larger picture of love.

Evaluate

5. Repeat-after-me prayer:

6. What are some tiny moments in your life? Send me what you discover.

A Little Context—A Life-Changing Gesture

As the sermon above notes, small expressions contribute to a larger creation. Bishop Desmond Tutu wrote of how a seemingly small act by an adult had a life-altering influence on him.

- "I believe the most defining moment of my life occurred when I was about nine years old, outside the Blind Institute in Roodepoort (South Africa) where my mother was a domestic worker. We were standing on the step when this tall white man in a black cassock, and a hat, swept by. I did not know that it was Trevor Huddleston. He doffed his hat in greeting my mother.

- "I was relatively stunned at the time but only later came to realize the extent to which it had blown my mind that a white man would doff his hat to my mother. It was something I could never have imagined. The impossible was possible.

- "I subsequently discovered that this was quite consistent with Trevor Huddleston's theology: that every person is of significance, of infinite value, because they are created in the image of God."

Trusting Our Support

This sermon works well for a streaming service.

Useful when...emphasizing that we are not alone.

Theme

You are not alone. Life works better when we have support.

Resources

Building blocks

Engage

1. Start building a precarious building and talk as you build.

    *   Hey, kids. You ever have times when you might feel alone and worry about things? I sure do. I bet there are a lot of grownups who do.

    *   We might feel like this building I'm making, all disorganized and— whoa!!!- It just fell over. Well, that's not a happy thing.

2. Let's rebuild this thing and make sure it has good support.

    *   First, some nice, big blocks for a stable foundation.

    *   Kind of like when we have someone we trust who loves us.

3. Keep building a sturdy building.

    *   Kind of like God reminding us we are loved and can love others.

    *   Do you know you are loved? I sure hope so. I hope you feel loved in our time together.

4. I'm imagining you and all your church friends who are watching now at home. I hope you feel connected with them.

5. Finish the nice, sturdy building.

    *   There, this one is a lot stronger. It has good support.

    *   Things always seem to work better when we have support.

Evaluate

6. Lead a repeat-after-me prayer giving thanks for support.

A Little Context—Be of Good Cheer

The sermon above explores the importance of having and trusting support in our lives. Support for children comes in many forms from adults. Some of it is formed by the church and then expressed in everyday life. Below is a story of how someone who was marginal in the larger society supported generations of children.

"Be of good cheer!" Steve's beloved Aunt Pearl always said to anyone who left her little house where she lived with her older sister, Nila. Steve had always thought it was some quaint, Appalachian saying she had brought from the Kentucky mountains. "Be of good cheer!" Or maybe it was from a Hallmark Card.

Twisted and bent by severe scoliosis, reduced in stature by a life-threatening childhood illness, Aunt Pearl served generations of nieces and nephews as a playful, loving measuring stick as they grew. Oh, to be as tall as she! They would have arrived. And then to be even a smidgen taller: they were destined for great things, and she would delight in their glee!

When their birthdays arrived, she sat that child on her knee and sang her special song to the tune of "What a Friend We Have in Jesus":

Happy Birthday Greetings to You.
May your future days be bright. May the
love of God's sweet sunlight Fill your life
with heavenly light. May God's presence
ever cheer you And God's blessings be your
store. Happy Birthday greetings to you And
we wish you many more.

Aunt Pearl had lived no cheery life. As a child, she had witnessed the deaths of three siblings: a sister at birth, a five-year-old brother from a fever, and a 14-year-old sister who "caught fire." She lived with fear during the coal mine wars of the early 20th Century as coal companies paid armed enforcers to break union organizing. With her older sisters and mother, she stopped her father as he beat her nine-year-old brother, who would become Steve's father.

She had lived life on an anvil and offered her tempered strength with a velvet touch. She sang hymns while cooking or doing dishes, knew swaths of the Bible by heart, and was strengthened by an extended family and the church.

"Be of good cheer!" It turns out she was quoting scripture from places where people suffered or were advocates for the vulnerable. "Courage, little ones!" is how Steve came to understand her encouragement.

When she died, all her earthly possessions fit in the bottom of a shopping bag: a commemorative church plate, her Bible, and some knickknacks. Ah, but her real treasure is scattered across the earth within untold numbers of grown-up children and the ones whom they encourage.

Theme: Otherness

Children learn that there are other people in the world with interests and needs. Children learn ways to connect with and express love for others.

A Board Game

Useful when...recognizing how the church is building a house for a family. Note: By focusing on the board, the dwelling, and the children's help in this process, you can avoid making this a commercial for the church.

Theme

How we express love.

Resources

- A 2 x 4 x 8 board
- Colored markers
- Someone to receive the board from the children at the end of the sermon.

Engage

1. Who here lives in a tree? A box? On the roof?
2. Where?
3. What are some things you like about where you live?
4. Some people need a place to live
5. Some of our adults are helping to build a house for a family who needs one.
6. Would you like to help?
7. You can sign this board or draw a picture of love on it. This board will become part of their house.
8. In Matthew 25 Jesus reminds us that, whenever we help someone who is thirsty or needs clothes or is hurting, we are doing it as if we are doing it for him.

Evaluate

9. How will people feel to have a house?
10. How do you feel about helping them?
11. Prayer
12. As they go to church school, the children carry the board down the center aisle and out of the sanctuary. Be sure to get it to the team that's working on the house.
13. Plan to have photos taken of the board as it's built into the house and of the finished house, as well. Be sure to share the photos with the children.

Good and Pleasant

This sermon works well for a streaming service.

Useful when...this Psalm supplements the worship theme.

Theme

Psalm 133:1 "How good and pleasant it is when people live together in unity."

Resources

Handbells and players

Engage

1. Hey, kids! You see what we have here?

   Handbells. Right.

2. What happens if you ring one of them? A single sound. Good.

3. Now, what happens when people come together and each one plays one?

   More sound. Pretty sounds.

4. Want to hear what it sounds like?

   - To bell ringers: Would you play a chord for us?
   - Chord sounds.

5. Look what happens when a bunch of bells work together.

   - Beautiful.
   - It is much better when we work together.

6. In the Bible, there is a verse that gives thanks for when we work well together.

7. Want to learn it with me? Okay. We'll do a repeat-after-me verse:

   - How good and pleasant it is
   - When people live together
   - In unity.

Evaluate

8. This week, look for times when people work together and let us know what you see and how it feels. Is it good and pleasant sometimes?

9. Repeat-after-me prayer:

   - Thank you, God.
   - For when we work well together.
   - For good and pleasant times
   - Amen.

A Little Context—On the Pain of Raising Children

Wisdom from Tzippy Cohen

"There is a Jewish saying/concept translated literally as "the pain of raising children" (*'tza'ar gidul banim'* צער גידול בנים). Any parent is familiar with that in a literal way. But I once heard it explained further to say that, yes, raising, disciplining, and guiding children is often a difficult, painful task.

"But what's most difficult is that in so doing we must also discipline and guide ourselves, raising our own standards so that we can step up to the parental plate and maintain our roles and composure even when the going gets tough.

"We experience our own growing pains in doing this and hopefully become better people and wiser at the same time too."

This can certainly describe our own growing pains as we learn to trust ourselves with children and develop our relationship with them and the adults during a children's sermon.

Hugs

Useful when connecting the children to the needs of others.

Theme

Expressing love

Resources

- Stuffed animals
- The choir to sing while the children bless the stuffed animals
- Someone to receive the basket(s) of stuffed animals at the end of the sermon.

Engage

1. To adults: Have you ever felt sad? Raise your hands if you are comfortable sharing.
2. To children: Do you ever feel sad? I hope it helps you to know that you are not alone.
3. Today we are going to bless some special friends before they leave on a very important trip.
4. Hold up a stuffed animal.
5. Anyone here have one of these?
6. What name do you call yours?
7. Anybody ever hug their stuffed animal?
8. How does that feel?
9. Well, there are children in another part of the country who are feeling sad. (Show the location on a map if possible.)

10. We've been invited to send them stuffed animals so they will know we are thinking about them.
11. Would you like to bless these stuffed animals for kids in another part of the country? (Ask the choir and congregation to softly sing something as the children bless each stuffed animal. A song like Jesus Loves the Little Children is a nice choice.)
12. Great! So, I'm going to start over here and hand the first one to you.
13. Your job is to hug each stuffed animal and, if you feel comfortable, whisper I love you in its ear.
14. Give it to the next person, who will do the same thing and pass it along.
15. Thank the children as you gather the animals in baskets. Explain that you will send these stuffed animals to children who have been feeling sad.

Evaluate

16. How do you think the children will feel to have one of these animals?
17. How do you feel helping?
18. Prayer
19. Children carry baskets down the center aisle and out of the sanctuary.

A Little Context—Catching Love

When Rachel was three years old, her beloved Papaw gathered his immediate family, grandkids and all, to talk with them about his memorial service. He knew that his yearslong relationship with leukemia was going to conclude his life in a matter of weeks. The family gathering didn't feel morbid at all; it felt more like a worship service as people offered their thoughts. Papaw quoted Tennyson, his favorite poet, "More things are wrought by prayer than this world dreams of." He was conveying that even as death is a part of life, it is not the final word to each of us.

Rachel was curled up on a couch with her special blanket, Bankie, which she took everywhere and clung to so ardently that, when anyone pretended to move it, she would crush it even closer to her. Her mother had to wait until Rachel slept before she could wash it.

Papaw grew weary and moved to the floor, where he rested on his side. The rest of the family continued to talk quietly about the service. At some point, one of the adults said, "Look very slowly," and gestured toward Papaw. Rachel was covering his shoulders very gently with her most cherished thing. Then she patted him and lay on the floor next to him. The room grew still as we savored this sacred moment.

Among the children who come running, skipping, walking toward you for the Children's Sermon, there may be, probably are, some who have caught how to love by the example of others and because they are formed to express it. They are ministering people. And they gather and look to you to encourage them.

Thirsty

Useful when...connecting the children to the needs of others.

Theme

Expressing love with water.

Resources

- Bottles of water
- Group that is taking water to thirsty people

Engage

1. When it's really, really hot and you've been playing outside, what do you like to drink?

2. Do you get your own drink or does somebody help you? Who?

3. What's it like when they give you something to drink?

4. Would you like to help somebody feel like that?

5. (Hold up bottle of water) What is this?

6. You think it would be a good thing to drink when you're thirsty?

7. See those people over there? (Invite them to come to center of chancel.)

    - They are going to take these water bottles to Arizona and give them to people who are crossing the desert. They are trying to find a new place to live.

    - Would you like to bless this water and these people as they go to help people?

8. Remember how we blow our Breath when someone is baptized. Remember the word? *Ruach.*

    - The Breath of God is in each of us.

    - So, we Breathe it on these water bottles and on these people to bless them on their way.

    - We remember that the people they will help also have the Breath of God in them.

9. In Matthew 25, Jesus reminds us that, whenever we give a thirsty person something to drink, we are giving it to Jesus.

Evaluate

10. Arrange for photos to be taken of giving the water bottles to thirsty people. Show them to the children, either in a future children's sermon or during church school.

A Little Context—Anonymous Helping

The sermon above shows the children how they can help people they may never meet. This quality of anonymous helping can have a significant impact, as the following story suggests.

There is a story of a government worker, John, who once rescued a young widow and her two children by doing nothing. A curious irony.

John had spent the night with cousins in Richmond, Indiana, so he could be in court by 10 the next morning. His cousin remembers that John arose that morning, shaved, put on his suit and tie, had breakfast, and then remained at the kitchen table. He poured a second cup of coffee and slowly leafed through the morning paper. John's cousin recalled:

It got to be 9:15, then 9:30, then 9:45. I said, "John, it takes about 15 minutes to get to the courthouse."

"'I know," he replied, as he took a sip of coffee and started reading another page of the paper.

Ten o'clock came and went and he was still at the table.

At about 10:15, I said, "John. You missed your appointment. That's not like you. Why didn't you go?"

John told me, "There's a woman at the courthouse with two children. She's at a hearing to determine whether she qualifies for her husband's survivor benefits. Because I didn't appear, she will get the benefits. If I had testified, I would have had to tell the court that she was not actually married to that man. She and their children would lose their survivor's benefits, and I would be responsible for ruining their lives. Having this coffee and reading this newspaper just seems like a better way to spend my morning."

At around 10:30 or 11:00, he left the house and returned to his office in Indianapolis.

He had bent the law and saved three lives—maybe more if you count into the future.

Whom does God love?

Useful when emphasizing that God loves everyone.

Theme

Jesus loves the little children of the world.

Resources

- Church-School Song: "Jesus Loves the Little Children"

- Choir and congregation

- "Let the children come to me, for of these are the realm of God."
  Matthew 19:14; Mark 10:13-16; Luke
  18:15-17

Engage

1. Hey kids, do you know a song about Jesus and little children?

    - (If they don't) Here's a clue: Jesus loves the little children…. Any ideas?

    - If they know it, ask them to sing it with you.

    - If they don't know it, ask the choir and congregation to sing it for and then with them.

2. So, does Jesus love only one kind of child?

    - How many different children does Jesus love?

    - Does Jesus love children with only one kind of skin?

    - Why do you think the song focuses on skin color?

3. So, which children does Jesus love?

Evaluate

4. Ask the children: If we pray for all children, what do you want the prayer to say?

    Gather their ideas, then lead a repeat after-me prayer.

5. Idea(s) for after the children's sermon:

    - Develop the point of the sermon in the church-school class.

    - Suggest that kids ask an adult to see how many different children they can find and think about how they are loved.

Theme: Spiritual

Children learn that there is more to life than we can see or understand. They learn that the sacred is part of everyday life that connects each of us to each other. They learn words the church has to try to describe these experiences.

A Little Context—Recovering Our Lost Humanity

Among the children who come to us and the adults listening in, there may be those who carry wounds they don't yet recognize. The following story shows how significant it is to have someone accompany us in our exploration of what separates us from our humanity.

In May 2001, an international, interfaith group of faculty, students, chaplains, counselors, and Holocaust survivors traveled to Poland. They called themselves The March of Remembrance and Hope. They came to learn together in the haunting places and memories of the Shoah. The haunting was made present to them as one afternoon some of them worked with Polish youth in the town of Oswiecim (Auschwitz) to restore the Jewish cemetery that had been desecrated only days earlier.

At their closing luncheon in Warsaw, Solange, a student from Canada who had grown up in Rwanda, came forward to speak. She had asked Sylvia, a Holocaust survivor, to stand with her. Solange began to speak,

"When I was a child in Rwanda in 1994, I hid under a table to keep from being killed by the Hutu. I could hear the screams of my family and friends outside as they died from machete blows.

"I was taken to safety in Canada. I thought I could cry there but no. And then I came on this trip and met Sylvia Guttman and she told me that she did not tell of her experience until 1992. Hearing this gives me hope that I, too, might one day find my lost humanity."

In the company of what Albert Schweitzer called the community of those who bear the mark of pain, we are beckoned. We are beckoned to be about the impossibly possible work of recovering lost humanity with others and maybe in the process for ourselves.

Finding God

This sermon works well for a streaming service.

Useful when...introducing the story of Jacob's Ladder and inviting children to think about when and where they feel close to God.

Theme

We want to be close to God.

Resources

The Children
A tall step ladder
Genesis 28: 10-17 – Jacob's Ladder

Engage

Start the sermon with one person standing on the floor and one person at the top of the ladder.
Show both people on a split screen.
Have a conversation, something like below:

Evaluate

Hey, Kids! Send us pictures and stories and ideas of how you have felt close to God.

LEFT SCREEN	RIGHT SCREEN
What are you doing up there?	Trying to get close to God. See if I felt closer to God up here. I heard that Jakob in the Bible had a dream about a ladder up to God.
How's it working?	I don't feel any different, except a bit dizzy.
What if you climb twice as high?	I would feel twice as scared, but not any closer to God.
Maybe finding God depends on where you are standing and how you are looking.	So, it depends on my point of view?
Good. I bet if the kids were here, they would say things like they sense God with them when they are in church or in the mountains or when they help someone or when the feel loved.	So, I don't have to climb high up this ladder to do that.
Only if you like to feel dizzy.	

Lighting the Dark

This sermon works well for a streaming service.

Useful when...we focus on God's light through the experience of love.

Theme

We find God's light and share it through the experience of love.

Resources

- The week after Easter
- A dark place at Church, like the boiler room.
- A flashlight.

Engage

1. Start in the boiler room, in the dark.

   "Hey kids! It sure is dark in here. I'm in the boiler room at church. Sometimes it can be scary in the dark. I wonder if it was like this for Jesus when he was in the tomb. I sure hope it gets light soon."

2. Turn on flashlight and shine it on your face.

   "Ah, this is better. Do I look spooky? One of you told me that you stood in front of a mirror, put a flashlight in your mouth and you could see your brain. Can you see my brain?"

3. Put lighted part of flashlight in your mouth.

4. "Could you see my brain? Let me know."

5. "We say in the church that God's light shines in the darkness. Can you think of times when someone's face lights up when they feel loved? I always felt that way when my dog came running to welcome me home. Maybe, when we feel loved or when we love someone, that is God's light. You become God's light in the world when you are loving."

Evaluate

6. "Today and during this week, would you look for ways that love lights up your face or the face of someone else? Let me know what you discover."

7. Repeat-after-me prayer giving thanks for the ways in which the children will see and be the light of God's love.

8. Later, share any insights the children send about love lighting up people's faces.

A Little Context—Being the Light

The sermon above encourages the children to be the light of love in the world. It's never too early to learn nor too late to express love. We never know when and how we will be called upon to be loving. So, we practice it at church, trusting that we will be ready when the time comes. This vignette below shows how a minister and a rabbi expressed love for each other and included children in that love. In this time of increasing and intense expressions of antisemitism and all manner of hatred toward other people, the encounter below offers a poignant model for how children learn that love is a powerful bridge.

In late Winter, 1957, Steve was part of what was called The Minister's Class at Erlanger (Kentucky) Christian Church. Ten-year-old kids met with their beloved minister each week to prepare for baptism and their first Communion on Maundy Thursday. Rev. Bowen used the symbols in the stained-glass windows to introduce important elements of the church, such as Spirit and prayer. He emphasized how God is love and that we know love because others have loved us.

One week, our group went to a synagogue in Cincinnati, Ohio. Steve remembers his feelings even these many years later:

I can't remember a thing that was said on that visit. But I will forever remember the joy with which my minister and the rabbi hugged each other and how the rabbi warmly greeted each of us in turn. I couldn't have told you then what was happening, but I now know that I was witnessing how love bridges indifference and hatred.

New Life

This sermon can work well in a streaming format.

Useful when emphasizing that the Easter theme of a return of life.

Theme

At Easter we celebrate the return of life.

Resources

- Easter eggs placed around the church grounds
- Daffodils in bloom

Engage

1. Invite the children to help you find Easter eggs. Ask them to tell you from home where to find them.

2. As you stroll along and come upon the eggs, ignore the eggs, and ask, "Am I getting warm? No?" and keep strolling.

3. Come to the daffodils and remark, "Look what's here, kids! Daffodils!! Aren't they pretty?!?"

4. "Sometimes when we are looking for one thing, we are surprised by something else that is beautiful.

5. Today we're walking along looking for Easter eggs, and we see these beautiful flowers. Then, all of a sudden, Wow! We are welcomed by new life, by the return of life.

6. Happy Easter, Kids!!"

Evaluate

7.   Suggestion: A Repeat-after-me prayer
giving thanks for new life.

A Little Context—Healing Gnomes

As the sermon above explores, we may find new life as a surprise gift. It encourages those who listen to watch for the presence of new life. The following vignette shows how a seven-year-old imagined the presence of new life as his grandmother was dying.

How does a seven-year-old respond to the passing of her beloved Nana?

Sofia envisioned that each of our bodies is filled, filled full of what she calls *healing gnomes*. When we get a cut, they rush there to start the healing. When we have a cold, they rush to push it out of our noses. And now, as her beloved Nana is dying, she says:

> Well, Nana's healing gnomes are packing up, so they don't have the time to rush around. They know she is dying and she won't need them anymore. They are packing up and, when she dies, they will leave and start their healing in a newborn baby.

Opening to God

Useful when wondering about being close to God.

Theme

God wants to come near to us, and we want to come near to God.

Resources

The chancel stairs

Engage

1. Let's keep standing until everyone is up here.

2. When all have arrived and you have greeted each one, point to the chancel stairs and ask: "Do these stairs go up or down? Take your time."

3. Look at the steps in silence.

4. "Before you decide that you're sure of your answer, let's try something together. First, let's go down the steps. Now, let's go up the steps."

5. "What do you think? Do they go up or down?"

6. Chances are one of the children will say, "Both!"

   - If not, then ask, "Did we go up or down the stairs just now?"
   - "Both? Right."
   - "Maybe it's that way with God.
   - What do you think?"

7. Walk up and down the steps as you ask:

   - God wants to come near to us and needs us to approach God?

   - We want to come near to God and need God to approach us?

Evaluate

9. What are some ways that God approaches us?

   Nature? Prayer? Friendship?

10. What are some ways that we approach God?

    Nature? Prayer? Friendship?

11. What have we learned today?

12. How can we use it?

13. Repeat-after-me prayer.

14. Reinforce the theme in church school.

A Little Context—Will God Always Be One?

As the sermon above expresses, we can trust children to imagine their way into important questions and dilemmas. We often marvel at what they remember and how they interpret what they hear at church, shown in this conversation.

While driving on a shade-dappled street, Steve heard a foundational question from his five-year-old daughter, "Daddy, will God always be one?"

It's amazing how swiftly the mind can race when presented with such an inquiry.

"What a wonderful question," I replied, in part to make it safe for her to keep thinking and asking questions. In part to give me time to craft a response.

"O, my!" I thought. "My response can shape her understanding for life. Does she catch the vision of the mystical union of all things—God as a unifying spirit?

"Or does she want to discuss where God's oneness refers to the monotheism versus polytheism tension when the text was compiled?"

Will God always be one?

I dare not tell her that, no, God isn't the only one. There are many gods that tear at those who maintain a beloved community,

- The God of war
- The deity of greed
- The transcendence of fear
- The holiness of mindless certainty

She'll discover these in her own time. Hopefully, she will find a community that will provide psychological safety and intellectual humility to explore her questions.

A spirit of listening, some might say sanity, came upon me and I responded, "Would you help me understand your question? Maybe ask it in a different way?"

"Will God always be one!?" She urged. "Won't God ever get to have a birthday and be two?"

The sound of my relief in that moment can still be heard wafting around the universe. "A fine question. What do you think?"

"I think God can have a birthday."

"Excellent. I look forward to hearing more of your questions."

A generational shift was occurring. It was my responsibility with others, not to provide ready answers, but to foster the crafting of questions within a caring community.

And in that moment, when graduate school met a five-year-old, there was oneness.

A Step and a Prayer

Useful when...emphasizing the importance of finding a quiet place to pray.

Theme

Take a step back and pray.

Prayer (Luke 5:15-16) [15] Yet the news about him spread all the more, so that crowds of people came to hear him and to be healed of their sicknesses. [16] But Jesus often withdrew to lonely places and prayed.

Resources

A self-effacing story about moving

Engage

1. Hey kids! Anybody here good at moving? Lifting things?
   - I'm great at lifting things, but not so great at getting things through the doorway.
   - So, yesterday, I moved a couch with some friends.
   - Things went great until we had to move it through a doorway.
2. How do you think that worked?
   Right! It got stuck!!
3. First, I shoved and pushed and grunted.
   You think that worked? No!
4. Then, I called someone.
   She said, "Tip it, then it will go right through."
5. What do you think happened?
   Right. It went right through.

Evaluate

8. What word or idea stands out for you?

   - Took a step back

   - Prayer

9. When can we do that, take a step back?

   Anytime and anywhere.

10. Repeat-after-me prayer.

11. Reinforce the theme during church school opening or as a focus of learning.

A Little Context—Study as a Form of Prayer

The sermon above shows the importance of finding a time and place to be open to the sacred. One way in which this can be possible is through the act of study. The following vignette shows how a certain youth spent time alone studying and came to a deeper understanding of love.

In youth group one Sunday evening, they were talking about God. A quiet, unassuming boy, said, "I have been reading the Bible. It says that God is love. Maybe, when we show love, we experience God in some way."

Wonder and Awe

Useful when introducing the experience of wonder and awe.

Theme

Noticing wonder and awe

Resources

A candle (preferably on the Communion table or altar) that casts a shadow onto the floor or wall

Engage

1. Show the children the lit candle.

2. Focus on the flame and ask what things the light does.

3. Go to the place on the floor or wall where the shadow of the candlestick is visible.

    *   (You may have to use a light to create the shadow.)

4. Ask where the shadow of the flame is in the shadow.
5. Draw their attention between the lit candle and its shadow.

6. Ask whether anybody else finds this to be amazing?

7. Note that when we are amazed like this, we say we are in awe. Like some of you when your eyes grew wider, and your mouths opened.

Evaluate

8. Are there other things that leave you feeling in awe? The mountains? A puppy? What else?

9. Would you do something this week? Remember one awesome thing that happened this week and let me know. Would you do that?

10. Repeat-after-me prayer marveling at being in awe.

11. Develop the theme in church school.

A Little Context—Healing

As the sermon above illustrates, children understand the experience of being in awe. Adults sometimes experience awe as a result of overhearing a children's sermon. Consider this story about a woman who was in awe at the gift she experienced from overhearing the children's sermon.

After worship one Sunday, an older woman came through the line to greet the minister.

It was clear that she had been crying.

The minister asked if she was okay.

"Yes. Yes," she said. "These are tears of gratitude. When I was a child, all we heard was that God hated us because of what we did. Today, when you told the children that God loves them, it was as if you were telling the child in me from long ago.

"And I believed it!"

Theme: Worship

Steve was sitting in church in 2003 a few weeks after his mother had died. It was as if they had chosen all her favorite hymns. He started to sing the first one but began to cry. Same thing with the next hymn. He was silenced by his loss. Then he heard the voices of others singing all around him and thought: "We sing on behalf of those who are silenced by loss, even as we trust that others will sing for us when we are silenced."

We provide children's sermons in worship, in part, so that children will know that they are part of a larger community of nurture.

A Little Context—Prayer Comes in Many Forms

Like the notes from a pipe organ, prayer comes in many forms. Sometimes the harmony of insight and discovery that children express shows us this variety.

"Love is like a campfire burning. If you don't tend it, it will go out." This is from the first sentence of a young person's confirmation speech.

"The blues tell the truth about life. Pop music tries to sugar-coat life. Not the blues. That's why you feel better after you hear them." Anonymous 15-Year-Old

Opening the Gifts of Worship

Useful when…celebrating the various components of worship.

Theme

Each part of worship is a gift.

Note: This lesson is great when Christmas is on a Sunday (or within a day either way).

Resources

Preparation

- If Christmas is on a Sunday, invite everyone to wear their jammies to worship.

- Type the name of each part of worship on a separate piece of paper, for example, Christmas Carol, Prayer, Call to Worship, Offering, Benediction, Announcements, etc. Include two or three pieces that say Christmas Reflection.

- Wrap each piece of paper and put them all in one gift box.

During the Service

- A random adult or two

- The gift box with the wrapped papers

Engage

8. Ask a child to pick a wrapped piece of paper from the gift box and to unwrap it.

9. Read what's on the slip of paper. Briefly say why this part of worship is a gift.

10. The minister, congregation, and the choir will then do whichever part of worship is on the paper.

11. When the gift says Christmas Reflection for the first time, ask if a child would like to tell of a favorite Christmas memory. For the second and third times, ask if an adult would like to share a favorite Christmas memory.

Evaluate

12. Ask if anyone sees worship differently after meeting each part.

13. Ask what they learned about worship.

14. Ask what it was like to hear the favorite Christmas memories that people offered.

15. Closer the service with a Christmas Carol.

Singing for Others

Useful when...emphasizing the importance of music in worship as empowering the community.

Theme

We sing for those who are silenced by sadness.

Resources

- Children
- A Song
- Musician
- Choir & Congregation

Engage

1. Hey kids, I have a really important question for you.
   - Sometimes when I'm sad, I feel a hurt inside. Like right here (point to heart)
   - Any of you ever feel that way when you are sad?
2. What kinds of things cause that kind of hurt?
   Suggestions: being left out, an unkind word, what else?
3. What is that like? Do we feel alone? Like we're the only one who feels that way?
4. Do you think anyone else in here has felt hurt?
   - Anyone want to ask them? (Point to the adults in the pews and the choir.)
   - Have you ever felt hurt inside? Raise your hand if you have.
5. So, the first thing is, if other people feel that way, maybe we're not alone. Ya think?
6. Sometimes people feel so hurt that all they can do is sit there and hurt.
   Sometimes they may even find themselves sitting in here or downstairs, feeling so hurt that they can't even talk or sing.
7. Well, who will sing for hurt people when they can't even sing?
   - Other people? What other people? Us?
   - So, is that one reason we sing? We sing for people who are silenced by hurt.
8. What about when we are so hurt that we can't sing? Who will sing for us?
   Other people?
9. So, we sing for people who are silenced by hurt.
10. We trust that others will sing for us when we are silenced.
    When we do that, we love one another.

Evaluate

11. Close with a song. Here are a couple of options:
    - "Jesus Loves Me"
    - "Strong Gentle Children

A Little Context—Comfort

The sermon above invited the children and adults to think about how they sing on behalf of those who are silenced by loss, even as they trust they someone will sing for them when they are silenced. The story below shows us the extended gift from one generation to another of this expression.

Alan Cole had the funeral of a woman who had a five-year-old son. At a certain point in the service, he moved from the pulpit and came and sat on the chancel stairs. He was at eye-level with the little boy in the front pew.

"It isn't easy having your mommy gone."

Gesturing toward the adults in the pews, he said:

> "There are people here who love you, like your aunt and your cousins and their families.
>
> "They want to be with you.
>
> "When I was five, my mommy died. It hurt and I missed her so much. Now I am here with you to let you know that there are people who loved me when I was sad, just like there are people who will love you when you are sad."

At that, the little boy left his pew, came to Alan, buried his face in Alan's chest, and hugged him tightly.

Note: We offer this as a poignant example of the power of a children's sermon, not as a recommendation. The moment seemed right to Alan, plus he has a gift for connecting with people in pain. Not all of us have that. If we misread the moment, we might make an object of a grieving child or put them in a very uncomfortable situation. So, we trust that you will savor this story and bring your best judgment to such a moment if you encounter it.

How to Pray

Useful when...learning how to pray.

This sermon works well for streaming.

Theme

Prayer is talking with God about what's on your mind.

Resources

- Pipe Organ
- Organist

Engage

1. Hey, kids!

2. I'm here with a bunch of organ pipes. Little bitty ones all the way up to giant ones.

3. The organist presses a key that looks like a piano keyboard, and it sends air through the pipes.

    - Each pipe plays a different note.
    - The small pipes play high notes. (Organist plays).
    - The big ones play low notes. (Organist place a 32-foot pipe)
    - If you were here, you could feel your clothes vibrate.

4. Walk toward the organist at the keyboard.

    - So many pipes. It looks complicated. But it isn't mysterious. We know how it works.
    - When we get to the organist, we'll see if she will play something for us.
      Okay. We're here. Would you play something?
    - The organist plays something fun, maybe by Charles Ore, like. "Jesus Loves Me."
    - To organist: Wow! And thank you!
5. Playing the organ seems pretty complicated, but it isn't mysterious. A person can learn to do it.

6. It's like that with prayer, only, unlike playing the organ, there's almost no way to do it wrong. Well, it's not like writing to Santa Claus with your Christmas wishes. Prayer is talking with God about what's on your mind. Anything that's on your mind. One person wrote a book that says that prayer is about help, thanks, and wow.

    - Asking for help.
    - Giving thanks.
    - Being amazed.

Evaluate

8. Have you tried talking with God? Let us know this week.

9. Repeat-after-me prayer.

Theme: Humor

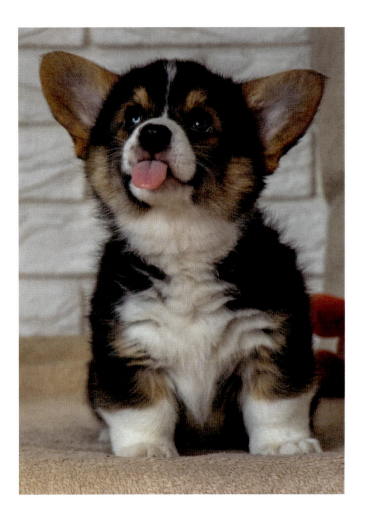

We think that, precisely because children experience great loss and sadness, it is important to provide occasions for laughter in church. In the sermons that follow, children will experience laughter: adults poking fun at themselves, playful interpretations that invite the insights of children, experiences that connect the tradition with enjoyment.

A Little Context—Through the Eyes of Children

As the sermons in this section invite, laughter can be a form of trust-building and nurture, provided it is not at the expense of someone else. If you provide a children's sermon, you will be well-served to learn about how children see life. This will enhance your ability to understand what tickles them, how they tease each other, and how they see the world. Below is a sampling of life through the eyes of children.

Nine-year-old sister to two-year-old sister: Can you say 'ah'? Two-year-old: (silence)
Father: What are you doing?
Nine-year-old: I wanted to see if she could say a vowel. 'A' is a vowel, right? Two-year-old: Vowel.

Six-year-old daughter to father: Can you look up "appropriate for six-year-olds scary shark pictures" on your phone and see if there are any that you're willing to show me?

Six-year-old daughter telling a story: "...and on the millionth floor of the T-Rex's treehouse is the nothingness."

Baby sister: <baby noises>
Seven-year-old sister: No. you can't go back into the uterus, silly.
Baby sister: <baby noises>
Seven-year-old: Well, fingernail cutting can hurt a little, but not too much.
Baby sister: <baby noises>
Seven-year-old: Sorry, sister, most of those things are impossible, and the rest will have to wait until tomorrow.

Three-year-old daughter: Where is your imagination—like where in your body?
Father: That's a good question. where do you think it is?
Three-year-old: Your head. Boy, there are a lot of things in your head: skull, brain, imagination, mind. I think the imagination is right behind the eyes. That way when you close your eyes, you can see what you're imagining.

Three-year-old daughter: Why is that train going on the tracks?
Father: Well...that's where trains go. Have you ever seen a train on the road? That'd be pretty silly, wouldn't it?
<pause>
Three-year-old: Do you know what a streetcar is?

A Guide

Useful when...inviting children to think about how we all need guides in our lives.

Theme

We all need a guide in our lives.

Nonverbal subthemes:

- People in authority sometimes make mistakes.
- Sometimes kids know best.
- You can have fun in church.

Resources

17. Ingredients and materials for chocolate chip cookies

- A rose (or other flower) on a stem instead of 2 cups of flour
- 1 cup of sand instead of 1 cup of brown sugar
- Container of mustard instead of butter
- 4 large hexagonal nuts instead of 1 cup pecans
- Dark Karo syrup instead of ½ tsp vanilla
- 1 chocolate chip in a small container
- 2 eggs
- A large mixing bowl
- A large mixing spoon
- Scissors
- A hammer (optional, but fun)
- A table
- An apron
- A chef's hat

18. Optional: Project slides that include the recipe and pictures of both correct and substitute ingredients. This is especially helpful if you are meeting in person.

Engage

19. Set up the table with the mixing bowl, large spoon, scissors, and hammer.
20. Ask, "Who likes chocolate chip cookies?"
21. Today I thought we'd make some chocolate chip cookie dough. Whaddya think? Sounds good, doesn't it?
22. Pass out the ingredients to the children. Ask them to hold onto each ingredient until you ask for it.
23. Put on the apron and the chef's hat.
24. One at a time, as possible, invite the children to put their ingredients in the bowl.
25. **Flour.** First, we need flour. Who has the measuring cup with the flour? Ah, you do! Take the measuring cup. Put the rose in the bowl (or ask the child to do this).
26. **Stem.** Wrong? Oh, yes, I forgot to cut off the stem. Cut off the stem and put the flower in the bowl.

27. **Brown Sugar.** Now we're supposed to put in the brown sugar. But since I don't have any today, I brought some sand, which is about the same color as brown sugar. OK? Who has the sand? Would you pour the sand in the bowl with the flower?

28. **Butter.** Now it calls for butter. But I don't have any of that, so I brought something from my refrigerator that is yellow, just like butter. Who has the mustard? Squeeze the mustard into the bowl.

29. **Nuts.** Nuts. Who has the nuts? Must have nuts. Pecans are too expensive. It's cheaper to use these hexagonal nuts. Hold up a nut so that everyone can see. Add the nuts to the bowl.

30. **Vanilla.** Let's see, now we need to add the vanilla. I don't have vanilla. Who has the Karo syrup? See, it's the same color. Have the child pour some in the bowl.

31. **Chocolate Chips.** Now it's time for the chocolate chips. I only have one, so I'll put it in now. Would you like to do that for us?

32. **Eggs.** Great! We're almost done! Now what? Eggs! Who has the eggs? OK, here are the eggs. I have some of those. Take the eggs and drop them into the bowl, shell and all.

    - OK? Kids will say No, you have to break them!

    - Oh, you're right. Thank you. With that, use the hammer (or a big spoon) and smash the eggs with the shells and stir them in.

33. **Check the Results.** OK, this will make some great cookies, won't it?

    - NO!

    - Why not?

    - You didn't put in the right stuff.

    - Ah, how would I know to do that?

34. Advice if You are Streaming the Service

    - Interact with statements like "Betcha didn't expect that!" or "I'll bet you were thinking those would…"

    - Watch Dan Ackroyd's impersonation of Julia Childs on Saturday Night Live for a great example of overplaying a cooking sequence.

    - Let them see your feigned outrage of things not working out.

Evaluate

35. Set up the idea of having a guide.

    - What did we learn? Do any of you want me to make cookies for you?

- What do we need when we do things? A guide? In this case, we could follow a recipe or ask someone for help who knows how to bake cookies.

- You all wanted to be my guide, didn't you?

- What kinds of guides do we have in church?

36. Lead a repeat-after-me prayer.

37. Reinforce the theme in an after-church session or in church school.

Finding Hope

Useful when looking for hope in difficult times.
This Sermon works well for streaming.

Theme

It's hard to find hope in a pandemic. Sometimes we just need a laugh.

Resources

- A stuffed animal (perhaps a monkey) to serve as a ventriloquist dummy
- Face masks for the two adults and the stuffed animal
- Corny jokes

Engage

1. Exchange greetings.

- **Adult 1**—What are you doing?
- **Adult 2**—I'm a ventriloquist. Here's my partner, George. Say 'Hi," George.
- **George**—Hi, George! Would you like to hear some jokes?
- **Adult 1**—Okay.

2. George tells a knock-knock joke.

- **George**—Knock! Knock!
- **Adult 1**—Who's there?
- **George**—Little Old Lady.
- **Adult 1**—Little Old Lady who?
- **George**—I didn't know you could yodel.
- **Adult 1**—Groan

3. George tells two Bible jokes.

Boaz & Ruth

- **George**—Who was Boaz before he married Ruth?
- **Adult 1**—I don't know. Who was Boaz before he married Ruth?
- **George**—He was ruth-less.
- **Adult 1**—Groan.

Solomon's Temple

- **George**—Here's another one. Where was Solomon's Temple?
- **Adult 1**—I don't know. Where was Solomon's Temple?
- **George**—On the side of his head!
- **Adult 1**—Groan

4. Wrapping up.

Adult 2—Sometimes it's hard to find hopeful things during this pandemic. So, we laugh together.

Evaluate

5. Hey kids! Send us your jokes. Especially Bible jokes.

6. Lead a repeat-after-me prayer.

Melting Away

Useful when…honoring that children will teach us important things if we let them.

Theme

Share what we have.

Resources

- A bowl full of small York Peppermint patties
- A glass of water

Engage

1. Hey, kids! Look what I have!

   Show them the bowl of mints.

2. Would you like to have some?

3. Carefully unwrap one mint, pop it into your mouth, and savor it with a big *Ummmm!*

   - Then fold the wrapper neatly and hand it to one of the children.

   - Children will no doubt look frustrated.

4. Repeat the process two or three more times. Ask one of the children to hold the bowl for you.

5. What's wrong?!?

   They will no doubt answer that you're supposed to share the candy.

6. Respond with "Oh, so we're supposed to share the candy now? Oh, well, that makes sense!!! It looks like there are still some pieces left in here. If you are allowed to have some, you can get one after we leave the sanctuary and go to Sunday School."

   You won't have to go into a moral or a Bible story. They get it.

7. Oh, and be sure to have a glass of water close by. After two or three Patties (not to mention four or five!), it's hard to talk with the ball of tasty goo in your mouth.

Evaluate

8. What did you learn today?

9. Lead a repeat-after-me prayer.

10. Reinforce the theme during church school opening gathering or make it the day's theme.

Sample Children's Sermon Template

Theme

What is the one (and only one) point you want to get across?

Resources

What resources will you use to convey the one point? (Don't forget the children themselves.)

Engage

How will you involve the children in learning about this one point?

Evaluate

During—How will you learn whether the children got your one point?
After—How will you reinforce your one point beyond the children's sermon?

Afterword

We offer you encouragement as you enter this important work of creating a covenant of care using children's sermons.

We have tried to show how children come to us with a whole assortment of thoughts and emotions, like curiosity and joy. They also bring their own yearning, their distinctive experiences of brokenness, and a sometimes-powerful sense of uncertainty. We have included examples of how adults who have encountered a children's sermon can sometimes gain a sense of consolation about unresolved losses in their lives.

We think of one occasion when even a second-hand recounting of one of these sermons brought meaning to a gathering of adults. One year (pre-Covid), Steve met with Regional Ministers of the Christian Church (Disciples of Christ) as part of their annual retreat. He spoke with them about the potential to create community using children's sermons in worship. He described the sermon found on page 34, *Ruach* –The Breath of God:

"We are about to baptize this person and we need your help. Would you gently blow your breath on the baptismal waters as a blessing for this child? As a gift to this child and family? By doing this, we're saying: you are loved. You are loving. Together we can be loving."

Steve invited the Regional Ministers to imagine themselves in that moment and gently blow their own breath as a gift to each other, to their meeting together, and to the people and churches they serve.

These clergy often respond to some of the most heart-wrenching of difficulties in the church. And, as they gently blew their breath, wind, and spirit in front of them, Steve saw that several of them had tears forming in their eyes.

In that moment, they experienced the gift of an empathetic witness to their unspoken sense of yearning, brokenness, and wandering.

Thank you for all the ways in which you provide an empathetic witness to these young (and older) lives that are entrusted to you. We invite you to remember:

> In our brokenness is our mending,
>
> In our yearning is our finding,
>
> In our wandering is our courage to receive the unknown—
>
> If we are accompanied by even one empathetic witness.

May you have and be such a witness through your expression of children's sermons in the formation of a covenantal community.

Acknowledgments

We're happy to show our gratitude for all this much-needed help. Also, this is the closest way we have of canonizing someone.

This resource exists because of the work and insights of four people who would be described as "Keepers" in the old country (aka, Kentucky). These four (Nate Miller, Dawn Grace Renshaw, Ben Konecny, and Robb Carlson) inspired and formed the substance of this resource.

First Congregational Church/United Disciples Fellowship in San José, California

Nate Miller, who is gifted at getting the kids riled up to learn (see A Guide and Melting)

Dawn Grace Renshaw, who has intuitive gifts (see *Ruach*–Breath of God)

First Congregational Church in Greeley, Colorado

Robb Carlson, whose gentle ways draw kids in (see Together Apart)

Ben Konecny, who greets kids by name and pokes fun at himself (see A Step and a Prayer)

Nate Miller, who moved to Greeley and continued to inspire the kids (see Finding Hope)

Each one worked to create a covenantal relationship.

Great thanks to this church for permission to use their excellent tree logo.

And Many More

We also want to thank these people who offered insight, encouragement, and inspiration:

Barbara Brown Taylor. Ola Harrison, Marsha Moors-Charles, Tex Sample, and Erin Wathen, loving educators all, for writing thoughtful responses to this resource. They are each gems!!!

Brian Allain, founder of Writing for Your Life (writingforyourlife.com), who is as affable as he is visionary and who provided crucial advice and connections. I hope you will connect with his new project, Raising Kids for Good, which supports progressive churches to prepare children for life.

Jean Bruns, who has one of the most organized minds in the universe, responded to the paucity of our knowledge, and gave us her insights about the publishing business.

Alan Cole, who claims to know nothing, studied child development at the University of Pittsburgh, has an uncanny way of hearing the nuance of concern in people's lives, and provided A Little Context reflection along with his usual stellar questions and insights.

Tzippy Cohen, wise beyond her years, who contributed the insights about how being a parent forms the character of a child and also the character of that parent.

Bryant Cureton, who suggested the wonderful metaphor of Keeper of the Fabric.

Mary & David Hulac, who bring insight, humor, and compassion to their work and their parenting, and remind us that the teeming coterie of kids on the back pew of the balcony are savoring a rare gift: the chance just to be.

Carol Monhollen, who knew from childhood that she wanted to be an elementary school teacher. She lent her knowledge of teaching and children to this project. Plus, she does amazing eye rolls, having had ample opportunities when her husband, Dave, and his brother, Steve, are together.

Dave Monhollen, who celebrated his 60th birthday by climbing to the top of a 50-foot pine tree in the woods to savor life at that height during a high wind. He also regularly sits with people as they are dying. He knows about breath, wind, and spirit, as he put into words for us to share with you.

Sandy Monhollen (of blessed memory), who offered insights for this resource, reveling in the spontaneity of the kids she observed during five years of children's sermons in Greeley.

The Rocky Mountain Conference of the United Church of Christ, who trusted us to give a workshop at the 2018 Annual Meeting at the La Foret Conference & Retreat Center, Black Forest, Colorado. (Robb and Steve were impressed with themselves for staying indoors to lead the workshop when the forest was beckoning them.)

Robb's wife, Sara Schneider, his best friend, love of his life, and long-time co-conspirator in ministry to children, whose love for education, attention to detail, and encouragement and partnership bring life and joy to this project.

Heather & Christian Schulte, who have great professional skills in therapy and law and great vocational commitment to care for people, including the burgeoning lives of their three children. They have a rare gift of moving in and out of the lives of children with wry humor and generous support.

Barbara Brown Taylor (again), who, to feel like a kid, read an early draft of this resource while sitting under the elm tree she planted on their north-Georgia farm 35 years ago. Great thanks for our Zoom session bringing timely and significant insights, recommendations, and encouragement.

Karen & Wayne Trainor, educators and friends extraordinaire, who sparkle together and taught us how to ask kids questions that don't sound like an interrogation.

Our friends and colleagues who contributed to the Zombie page: Wes Allen, Anonymous, Jeanne Farrington, Stephanie Fuhrmann, Wanda Vasquez Garcia, David Hulac, Sandy Magnuson, Amanda Wagoner Meade, Cherri Metier, Stacey Nicholas, Mary Lu Strange, Tanya Tyler, and Mark Underwood.

The children who bring their lives to us, tell us important things, and beckon us into life.

We give special thanks and praise to Jeanne Farrington (Steve's beloved), who brought her many years of editing experience to this project. We now understand why authors lavish praise on the ones who take formless drafts, exclaim the occasional "What were you thinking?!?!?!" and offer recommendations to bring life to a project. Any mistakes in judgment are from Robb and Steve. Any formatting glitches are compliments of Microsoft. Brava to Jeanne, who started this project with little use for children's sermons and saw by meeting these examples how life-giving they can be.

Notes & References

Here are some references for quotations or similar works in this resource.

Introduction

Page 1 …we decided to try to picture "the thing with feathers that perches on the soul,"
Dickinson, Emily. "'Hope' is the thing with feathers."
https://www.poetryfoundation.org/poems/42889/hope-is-the-thing-with-feathers-314

Page 1 "We created this resource to share the work of clergy…"
Nate Miller and Dawn Grace Renshaw at First Congregational Church/United Disciples Fellowship, San José, California and the work of Robb Carlson, Ben Konecny, and Nate Miller at First Congregational Church, Greeley, Colorado. Alan Cole and Steve Monhollen, retired Disciples of Christ chaplains and ministers. These churches have safe church policies. For additional information, see
https://www.insuranceboard.org/wpcontent/uploads/2020/06/Safe-Conduct-Policy-Template.pdf

Page 1 "…a mixture of wry detachment and warm-spirited interest." Coles,
Robert. (1990). *The Spiritual Life of Children*. Houghton Mifflin.

Page 1 Abigail Johnson's book on shaping…
Johnson, Abigail. (2007). *Shaping Spiritual Leaders: Supervision and Formation in Congregations.* Rowman & Littlefield Publishers.

Page 3 We think it is important to receive another person with humility….
Cole, Rev. Alan. (November 14, 2021). Personal communication.

Page 3 We did our best to focus on the perspectives and experiences of the children…
For a brilliant example of how this is done, we encourage you to see the work of Robert Coles, who documented how children and their parents deal with profound change. You might start with *Children of Crisis: A Study of Courage and Fear*. Back Bay Books (1967). and *The Spiritual Life of Children*. Houghton Mifflin Company. (1990)

Anatomy of a Children's Sermon

Page 8 Adults often enjoy these moments…
Scott, Bernard Brandon, Vearncombe, Erin, Taussig, Hal. (2021). *After Jesus Before Christianity*. HarperOne. See pages 147-198.

Page 9 Use positive language...
Nucaro, Alyssa. "Positive Words Go a Long Way."
https://www.edutopia.org/article/positivewords-go-long-way

"Responsive Classroom. Want Positive Behavior? Use Positive Language."
https://www.responsiveclassroom.org/want-positive-behavior-use-positive-language/ **Page 10**
Strong, gentle children
Damon, Daniel Charles. (1993). "Strong Gentle Children." Hymn Text Words. Hope Publishing
Company.

How to Use This Resource

Page 11 People will care how much you know….
Versions attributed to President Theodore Roosevelt, John Maxwell, Earl Nightingale, and
others. https://coloradocommunitymedia.com/stories/its-not-how-much-you-know-
itsabout-how-much-you-care,253742

Story: The Central Energy of a Children's Sermon

Page 13 Tex Sample
Sample, Tex. (1994). *Ministry in an Oral Culture: Will Rogers, Uncle Remus & Minnie Pearl.*
Westminster John Knox Press. See pages 13-16 and 35-37.

Covenant: More Than Show, Glow, and Go

Page 14 A *covenant* is not the same as a contract.
Sacks, Jonathan. (2003). *The Dignity of Difference: How to Avoid the Clash of Civilizations.*
Bloomsbury. passim.

Page 14 Love themselves and others into life each day.
L'Heureux, John. (2002). *The Miracle: A Novel.* Grove Press. 93-94. In L'Heureux's book, the
priest realizes during his homily that, at the end of our lives, the one important question
we will be asked to account for our lives is this: Whom have you loved into life?

How to Avoid Creating Zombie Children

Page 19 Below are some wise insights...
These delightful responses came from Steve's Facebook invitation to friends.

Have Courage

Page 32 "I Am Somebody!"
Jackson, Jesse. Sesame Street – I Am Somebody.
https://www.youtube.com/watch?v=iTB1h18bHlY&t=1s

Examples of God's Breath

Page 36 When has God breathed on you recently?
Monhollen, Dave. (2020) Unpublished reflection

A Helping Witness

Page 39 ...children can be reassured...

Miller, Alice. "The Essential Role of an Enlightened Witness in Society." https://www.alice-miller.com/en/the-essential-role-of-an-enlightened-witness-in-society/

A Life-Changing Gesture

Page 41 ...small expressions contribute to a larger creation.

Tutu, Desmond. https://www.iol.co.za/capetimes/the-man-who-changed-my-life-1533199

Healing

Page 65 Beyond the strictly physical sense...

Hellwig, Monika. (1976). *The Eucharist and the Hunger of the World.* Paulist.

Helpful Resources

Here is a short list of resources that we find to be helpful. We encourage you to develop your own expanded list of resources that will help you in your essential work. You'll find general references and then a section to help when considering how to talk with children about traumatic events.

General References

Coles, Robert. (1967) *Children of Crisis: A Study of Courage and Fear*. Little, Brown and Company.

> Robert Coles invested his life as a psychiatrist in the study and care of children in their communities, receiving a Pulitzer Prize for this series. He emphasizes listening to the children and their parents and drawing on their insights to deepen his and their learning. We find this process to be very helpful when preparing sermons for children.

Coles, Robert. (1991). *The Spiritual Life of Children*. HarperOne; Reprint Edition.

> Robert Coles reminds us that children witness the full range of human experience and can teach us how to live honestly and courageously if we let them. We value this book because it strengths our own commitment to, as he puts it, respond to our learning about children with "...a mixture of wry detachment and warm-spirited interest."

Dickinson, Emily. "'Hope' is the thing with feathers."
https://www.poetryfoundation.org/poems/42889/hope-is-the-thing-with-feathers-314

> Emily Dickinson's reflection on hope seems well-suited to our exploration of the fragile yet tenacious spirit of what it means to create a covenant of care.

Hershovitz, Scott. (2022) *Nasty, Brutish, and Short: Adventures in Philosophy with My Kids*. Penguin.

> Hershovitz is director of the Law and Ethics Program and professor of law and philosophy at the University of Michigan. Sounds pretty stuffy. He also has two kids who ask perplexing questions (as they do). The result: this book, which is a delightful invitation to adults to learn the art of thinking with the help of the insights and questions of children. He can help you think about life's questions from the perspective of children.

Jackson, Jesse. Sesame Street – I Am Somebody.
https://www.youtube.com/watch?v=iTB1h18bHlY&t=1s

Johnson, Abigail. (2007). *Shaping Spiritual Leaders: Supervision and Formation in Congregations*. Rowman & Littlefield Publishers.

> Our TREE model comes from her method and her emphasis on starting with the question, "What do we want to learn?" You can learn more about applying her method to other parts of your work.

King, Maxwell. (June 8, 2018). "Mr. Rogers Had a Simple Set of Rules for Talking to Children." *The Atlantic.* https://www.theatlantic.com/family/archive/2018/06/mr-rogers-neighborhood-talking-tokids/562352/

> A must-read. The author describes what he calls Freddish, the special way in which Fred Rogers spoke with children. He shows you how to speak Freddish in nine easy lessons. This is a wonderful addition to our encouragement to use positive language with children.

Nucaro, Alyssa. "Positive Words Go a Long Way." https://www.edutopia.org/article/positive-wordsgo-long-way

> Practical advice for using positive language with children.

Responsive Classroom. Want Positive Behavior? Use Positive Language. https://www.responsiveclassroom.org/want-positive-behavior-use-positive-language/

> More practical advice for using positive language with children.

Sacks, Jonathan. (2020). *Morality: Restoring the Common Good in Troubled Times.* Basic Books.

> Rabbi Lord Jonathan Sacks (of blessed memory) was the Chief Rabbi for the United Kingdom. He wrote and spoke about the centrality of creating and maintaining covenantal relationships. This book is a fine introduction to his thought and will help you understand children's sermons as a way to create a covenantal relationship.

Sample, Tex. (1994). *Ministry in an Oral Culture: Will Rogers, Uncle Remus & Minnie Pearl.* Westminster John Knox Press. From Steve Monhollen's review: https://pcpe.smu.edu/blog/ministry-in-an-oral-culture-will-rogers-uncle-remus-and-minnie-pearlby-tex-sample

> Tex Sample devoted his intellectual work to bridging the divide between an intellectual and a communal approach to religion. He saw that the white, working-class culture of his upbringing has its own wisdom, moral integrity, and means of critique in a world of hard times.
>
> This small volume shows and tells us how story, proverbs, and relational thinking address life's hardness, explore society's brokenness, and, in a sense, exorcize despair. He invites us to draw from the language styles of working-class culture to energize our storytelling. This book can enrich your understanding of storytelling as a central focus of the lives of children.

Trauma and Children

NOTE: We recommend that you **not** focus on the specific traumatic event. It is possible that some parents are buffering their children from the trauma. We recommend inviting the children to explore how they are loved. Below are some resources to help you do that.

Holmes, Margaret M. (2000). *A Terrible Thing Happened.* Magination Press.

> A children's book that shows the importance of having even one person who will acknowledge a child's loss. See A Little Context—Comfort on page 71 for a poignant example of this encounter.

Karst, Patrice. (2018). *The Invisible String.* Little, Brown Books for Young Readers.

> Parents, educators, therapists, and social workers alike have declared *The Invisible String* the   perfect tool for coping with all kinds of separation anxiety, loss, and grief. In this relatable and   reassuring contemporary classic, a mother tells her two children that they're all connected by an   invisible string. "That's impossible!" the children insist, but still they want to know more: "What   kind of string?" The answer is the simple truth that binds us all: *An Invisible String made of love.   Even though you can't see it with your eyes, you can feel it deep in your heart, and know that   you are always connected to the ones you love.* Does everybody have an Invisible String? How   far does it reach? Does it ever go away? This heartwarming picture book for all ages explores   questions about the intangible yet unbreakable connections between us, and opens up deeper conversations about love.

Miller, Alice. "The Essential Role of an Enlightened Witness in Society."
https://www.alicemiller.com/en/the-essential-role-of-an-enlightened-witness-in-society/

> Dr. Alice Miller notes how having a helpful witness to a child's suffering, even later in adulthood, can transform a person. She focused on the impact of childhood trauma, writing seminal books, including, *The Untouched Key: Tracing Childhood Trauma in Creativity and Destructiveness* (1991).

National Child Traumatic Stress Network (2006). *Psychological First Aid PFA, Field Operations Guide*, 2nd Edition.
https://www.nctsn.org/sites/default/files/resources//pfa_field_operations_guide.pdf

> Provides a process for offering psychological first aid with children who have experienced trauma.

> Note: It's important to use a guide such as this in consultation with a mental health care professional.

Safe Church Conduct Policy. https://www.insuranceboard.org/wp-content/uploads/2020/06/Safe-Conduct-Policy-Template.pdf

> Several denominations have this kind of resource to help congregations develop safe church policies. These policies might include things like making sure there are two unrelated adults

with a group or when a child needs a ride home. Both First Congregational Church of Greeley, Colorado and First Congregational Church/United Disciples Fellowship of San José, California have safe church policies and practices.

Schulte, Heather. (2022) "Trauma informed practices." Conversation.

If someone presents a children's moment in the aftermath of a trauma (a shooting, tornado, death of a beloved person), it is important to become acquainted with the dynamics of trauma.

I recommend that you not focus on the specific event. It is possible that some parents are buffering their children from the trauma. I recommend inviting the children to explore how they are loved. The two books, *A Terrible Thing Happened* by Margaret Holmes and *The Invisible String* by Patrice Karst are wonderful resources to help you.

If possible, please consult a therapist for advice, let parents know in advance that you will be addressing a difficult thing in general, and provide resources for parents to use for their own support of their child or children.

I recommend studying the Window of Tolerance to become acquainted with the responses to trauma.

The main contribution you can make is to provide the children with a sense of safety, trustworthiness, a sense of support, and offer them choices of how they can respond. Better yet, invite them to identify how they feel loved, to suggest people with whom they feel safe, and to offer ideas about how they might find support and support others.

See Cole, Esther. (2020) "Expanding the 'Window of Tolerance'" Supporting children's ability to cope with anxiety. *Psychology Today*. https://www.psychologytoday.com/us/blog/lifespan-psychology/202004/expanding-thewindow-tolerance

Wust, MaryKate. (April 2, 2018). "It's an Emotional Day in the Neighborhood." Penn Medicine News. https://www.pennmedicine.org/news/news-blog/2018/april/its-an-emotional-day-in-theneighborhood

A poignant reminder of the importance of creating safe places for children where life slows down enough for everyone to just be. Insights from the work of Fred Rogers, who, by the way, was a Presbyterian minister with credentials from the Graduate School of Child Development at the University of Pittsburgh.

Picture Credits

Cover – Kids Cartoon—Image by Prawny from Pixabay
https://pixabay.com/illustrations/kids-children-cute-childhood-2030260/

Zombies—Image by Gordon Johnson from Pixabay https://pixabay.com/vectors/male-man-boy-zombie-undead-1781413/?download

Tell Me a Story—Image by 0fjd125gk87 from Pixabay
https://pixabay.com/illustrations/book-dog-fairy-tales-child-kid-794978/

Rainbow Tree – Logo, First Congregational Church, Greeley, Colorado. Used by permission.
https://www.firstconggreeley.com/

How Am I Doing? —Image by OpenClipart-Vectors from Pixabay https://pixabay.com/vectors/lion-animal-confused-bewildered-159448/

Squirrel—Image by Sammy-Sander from Pixabay https://pixabay.com/photos/squirrel-rodent-newspaper-reading-6374731/

Puppies - Image by Rajesh Balouria from Pixabay
https://pixabay.com/photos/newborn-pups-puppies-dog-cute-baby-5094468/
Image by JackieLou DL from Pixabay
https://pixabay.com/photos/dog-bitch-young-dog-puppy-2775015/

Belonging – Two Dogs Running—Photo by Alvan Nee on Unsplash
https://unsplash.com/photos/1VgfQdCuX-4

Keepers of the Fabric—*Salisbury Cathedral from the Bishop's Grounds* by John Constable c.1825.
https://commons.wikimedia.org/wiki/File:Salisbury_Cathedral_from_the_Bishop_Grounds_c.1825.jpg

Why? Image by Gordon Johnson from Pixabay https://pixabay.com/vectors/why-question-marks-unknown-ask-2028047/

A Terrible Thing Happened —Margaret Holmes—-Image from Amazon.com

Otherness – Snuggling Animals—Photo by Krista Mangulsone on Unsplash
https://unsplash.com/photos/9gz3wfHr65U

The Pain of Raising Children—Image by PDPhotos from Pixabay
https://pixabay.com/photos/sapling-rock-tenacity-tough-plant-3653/

Spiritual – Peacock Feather—Image by suji-foto from Pixabay
https://pixabay.com/photos/peacock-feather-macro-peacock-bird-3030524/

Worship – Goat kids jumbled around—Image by ludex2014 from Pixabay
https://pixabay.com/photos/goats-animals-goat-baby-animal-1301709/

Gifts of Worship—Image by blende12 from Pixabay
https://pixabay.com/illustrations/gift-packages-christmas-give-a-gift-2975401/

Humor – Cute dog—Image by <u>Elena Rogulina</u> from <u>Pixabay</u>
<u>https://pixabay.com/photos/tongue-corgi-welsh-corgi-pembroke-4902262/</u>

A Guide—Image by Clker-Free-Vector-Images from Pixabay <u>https://pixabay.com/vectors/squirrel-reading-books-surprise-304021/</u>

Finding Hope—Image by Christian Dorn from Pixabay
<u>https://pixabay.com/illustrations/pogen-dance-leap-pleasure-children-4846362/</u>

About the Authors

Steve Monhollen - Just as a song catches our imagination and shapes how we feel, think, and act, Steve Monhollen was caught by the way four ministers at two churches created a community of welcome through the weekly children's moment in worship. As he told other clergy and church members about this experience, they encouraged him to create a resource that could help them develop such a community. At a workshop where Steve and his collaborator, Robb Carlson, introduced the resource, one church member pulled Steve aside and said, almost in a whisper, "I hope you will publish this. Our minister could use some support."

Steve, having been around the ministerial block a bit as a local church minister, college chaplain, seminary professor, elder care minister, and adult learning provider, interviewed the four ministers and coaxed together a method for entering the realm of children's sermons. He consulted children, parents, educators, children's therapists, clergy, former students, a custodian, and others who brought insights into being present with children.

Steve also recognizes the limits of this resource: technique will seem empty unless it is combined with a spirit of wonder. He hopes that the methods and techniques of this resource help you trust yourself and the children and catch the wonder of learning with and for them.

Steve has degrees from Transylvania University, Vanderbilt University, and Hebrew Union College – Jewish Institute of Religion with a year of graduate studies at the Hebrew University in Jerusalem. He is Professor Emeritus of Pastoral Leadership, at Lexington Theological Seminary, Lexington, Kentucky. His most life-deepening gifts have come from being a spouse, father, grandfather, family member, friend, caregiver, patient, student, and teacher. He lives in San Jose, California with his wife, Jeanne, where they serve as staff for their three cats.

Robb Carlson creates a sphere of exploration for children and for the adults who overhear his conversations. He and Steve designed and provided a workshop on children's sermons at the Annual Meeting of the Rocky Mountain Conference of the United Church of Christ. Together, they have fine-tuned this resource. Robb is the Director of Religious Exploration at South Valley Unitarian Society, Salt Lake City, Utah.

Robb hails from northern Colorado and has served local congregations in the United Church of Christ for almost two decades in the area of children, youth, and family faith formation ministries. Robb holds a B.A. in philosophy from the University of Northern Colorado and is currently completing his thesis at the United Theological Seminary of the Twin Cities for a Master of Arts in Ethics & Justice. Robb has been involved in the leadership of numerous outdoor/camp ministry programs for children and youth as a camp counselor, camp director, retreat coordinator, song leader, and worship musician.

Made in the USA
Monee, IL
11 June 2024

59747709R00059